Rosalie,
May the memories of
Alaska's people and
your time in the north
live on!

Aunt Phil's Trunk: Volume I

An Alaska historian's collection
of treasured tales

By
Phyllis Downing Carlson
Laurel Downing Bill

Laurel Downing Bill
Christmas 2012

Aunt Phil's Trunk LLC

www.auntphilstrunk.com

The front cover design by Kristy Bernier of Palmer, Alaska, features Phyllis Downing Carlson, aunt of Laurel Downing Bill, prior to her death in 1993. Carlson grew up in Alaska and wrote numerous magazine and newspaper articles about the state she loved.

Also on the cover, from left: Eskimo hunter, George A. Parks Collection, Alaska State Library P-240-210; Mathison brothers, Sylvia Sexton Collection, Seward Community Library 1-798; prospector, Skinner Foundation, Alaska State Library P44-03-15; and shaman with totem, Case and Draper Collection, Alaska State Library P-39-782.

Robert DeBerry of Anchorage took the photograph on the back cover.

International Standard Book Number 978-1-57833-330-1
Library of Congress Control Number 2006908361

Printed and bound in U.S.A.

Third printing 2010

DEDICATION

I dedicate this book to Aunt Phil's stepchildren, grandchildren, great-grandchildren and their families; to Aunt Phil's sister, Jean Downing Anderson of Seward; to my brothers and sisters, their families and all our cousins. I also dedicate the work to my husband, Donald; son Ryan; and daughter Kim and her husband, Bruce Sherry. Thank you so much for believing in me.

Lastly, I dedicate this collection of historical stories to my first grandchild, Sophia Isobel Sherry, as her giggles and slobbery baby kisses kept me sustained through long hours while working on this project.

ACKNOWLEDGMENTS

I owe an infinite debt of gratitude to the University of Alaska Anchorage, the University of Alaska Fairbanks, the Anchorage Museum of History and Art, the Alaska State Library in Juneau, the Z.J. Loussac Public Library in Anchorage, the Seward Community Library and the University of Washington for helping me collect the photographs for this book. Without the patient and capable staffs at these institutions, the following pages may not have been filled.

I also want to extend a heart-felt thank you to Robert DeBerry of Anchorage for his excellent attention to detail as he readied for publication the majority of the historical photographs that appear in Volume I of Aunt Phil's Trunk. Thank you, too, to Ken Werning of Harlingen, Texas, for restoring a number of Aunt Phil's old photos. And I am extrememly grateful to Nancy Pounds of Anchorage for slaving away with her eagle eyes to carefully proof-read the pages.

My family deserves medals, as well, for putting up with me as I chased down just the right photographs to go with Aunt Phil's stories, poured over notes and the collection of rare books that make up Aunt Phil's library and sat hunched over my computer for hours blending selections of Aunt Phil's work with stories from my own research.

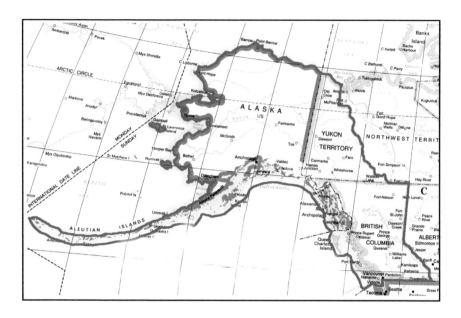

"Aunt Phil's Trunk: Volume I" tells of various adventurers who traveled through Alaska and the Yukon Territory of Canada, and includes stories up to the Klondike Gold Rush at the turn of the 20th century.

Phyllis Downing Carlson, who arrived in Cordova, Alaska, in 1914 at the age of 5, lived and loved the history about which she wrote.

FOREWORD

This book contains a collection of Alaska history stories written by my aunt, Phyllis Downing Carlson, as well as stories written by me that came from tidbits found among the notes and rare books I inherited when she died in 1993.

Born in 1909, Aunt Phil moved to Alaska in 1914 and lived the history so richly described in her work. She grew up in Cordova, where her father worked on building the railroad to the Kennecott copper mines; he then served as the conductor aboard the Copper River and Northwestern Railroad. Phyllis graduated with a class of seven from Cordova High School in 1928, then studied journalism at the University of Washington and earned a teacher's certificate from Central College of Education in Ellensburg, Wash.

Aunt Phil landed her first job, which paid a whopping $150 a month, at Cooper Landing on the Kenai Peninsula. The new teacher kept the Yukon stove stoked in the little log schoolhouse and worked around cases of milk and staples stored for the winter.

After three years in the isolated community of 30, a widowed father of three of her pupils put an end to her single days. Carl Carlson moved her to the village of Tyonek, across Cook Inlet from Anchorage, and Phil again taught school in 1935 while Carl ran the village sawmill and served as postmaster.

The young bride met Tyonek Chief Simeon Chickalusion, who spoke English, Russian and his Native tongue. She later wrote an article, titled "The Tribe That Kept Its Head," about the chief and residents of Tyonek that ranked as one of the best articles submitted in a 1967 Writer's Digest contest. Years later, the village invited her back to a potlatch to share stories of the chief with the village young people.

The Carlsons moved to Anchorage in 1939, where Carl helped build Fort Richardson. The couple pitched a tent at Fifth Avenue and Denali Street and started framing a house over the tent. When they completed their home, they took down the tent and dragged it out the front door.

As a child, Alaska historian Phyllis Downing Carlson skipped down these dirt streets in Cordova, pictured here in 1919.

Aunt Phil taught school in the Native village of Tyonek in 1935. The village looked much like this photograph taken in 1898. She befriended Chief Simeon Chickalusion and was invited back to a potlatch when the village relocated after the earthquake of 1964.

After World War II, the couple moved to Cordova, where Aunt Phil honed her journalism skills. She produced her own radio show, "Woman to Woman," and conducted countless interviews that eventually led her to research Cordova's history through the local newspaper's archives.

"Oh, I had a wonderful time," she later recalled. "They had a real storehouse."

Her popular radio show led to the compilation of entertaining articles about Alaska, and for more than 40 years, Aunt Phil researched and wrote award-winning pieces as she moved about the state. Her stories appeared in a multitude of publications, including Alaskana, Alaska Journal, Alaska Sportsman, The Anchorage Times and Our Alaska.

She settled back in Anchorage from Kodiak after the Good Friday earthquake of 1964, and spent so much time researching and talking with librarians at the Z.J. Loussac Public Library, they hired her. People said she didn't need to use the card catalog, because she knew the location of every volume.

"I don't remember faces," she said. "But I remember what I looked up for people."

The Alaska Press Women chose Aunt Phil for its Woman of Achievement Award in 1988. The organization cited her as an authority on Alaska history, recognized throughout the state by writers, researchers and politicians alike.

As a retiree, she served on a variety of boards, including the Anchorage Bicentennial Commission, Historical Landmarks Preservation Commission, State Historical Society and Alaska Press Women.

When she passed away in 1993, her treasured tales landed in my hands. As providence would have it, I, too, am a writer and lover of Alaska history. And since Aunt Phil was one of my favorite relatives, I feel it a privilege to perpetuate her work.

My Alaska roots stem from both sides of my family. My father, Richard Allie Downing – Aunt Phil's younger brother – was born in Cordova in 1916. Not only was his father a part of the railroad history there, but his grandfather, John Couch Downing, had witnessed the staking of gold claims around the area many years before when he sailed as the captain of the *Excelsior*, the famous steamship that carried news of the riches found in the Klondike back to San Francisco in July 1897.

My mother's grandfather, Robert Burns Mathison, arrived in Hope from Texas in 1898 and helped establish that little mining town. He pulled a small fortune out of Resurrection Creek and Chickaloon River and built a sawmill and mercantile. His son, Robert Lewis Mathison, married my grandmother, Inez Lee Brown, who traveled to the small community to work for her uncle, Charlie Shields, after being widowed in Kansas.

From that union came my mother, Hazel Isobel, and her identical twin, Hope Alisabeth, born at the Anchorage railroad hospital in 1920. The twins spent summers in Hope and winters in Seward, where they graduated high school in 1938.

My folks met at the University of Alaska Fairbanks, married in 1941, and settled in Fairbanks to raise their family. I was the fourth of their children born at old St. Joseph's Hospital, in 1951, following brothers Richard Ellsworth and Michael Woodrow and sister Meredith Lee.

I grew up between that gold-rush town and Juneau, where we moved after my father became the first commissioner of Public Works when Alaska became a state in 1959. That's where my younger sister, Deborah Lynn, was born in 1965 – shortly after my mother christened the Taku, the Alaska Marine Highway System's second ferry.

In 1973, I married and then spent 22 years in King Salmon with my fisheries biologist husband, Donald Bill. I worked for the Bristol Bay Telephone Cooperative Inc. and raised two children, Kimberly and Ryan, and a foster daughter, Amie Morgan.

When the children graduated from Bristol Bay High School, and Don retired from the Alaska Department of Fish and Game, we moved to Anchorage. I went back to school in 1999, at the tender age of 48, and learned that I had a passion for writing. I earned a bachelor's degree in journalism in May 2003 from the University of Alaska

Anchorage and have spent the past few years writing my own award-winning articles for various Alaska newspapers and magazines while working on this labor of love.

Condensed versions of articles in "Aunt Phil's Trunk" appeared in The Anchorage Chronicle, a weekly newspaper published by Alaska Newspapers Inc. from July 2002 until the paper closed its doors on Dec. 31, 2004. The Senior Voice, a monthly Alaska newspaper, picked up the column in February 2005.

I truly hope you enjoy this volume packed with Aunt Phil's articles and other stories that came from research jotted down in piles of notebooks, countless lined tablets and in the margins of rare books that make up "Aunt Phil's Trunk: Volume 1."

 – *Laurel Downing Bill*

Charles, left, and Robert L. Mathison, maternal grandfather of Laurel Downing Bill, walk away from the Pacific Coast Trading Company and U.S. Mineral Surveyor and Assaying Office in Seward around 1906. The brothers, who mined with their father, Robert Burns Mathison, prospected around the gold-rush town of Hope.

TABLE OF CONTENTS

DREAMS OF GOLD

RUSH TO THE KLONDIKE

SEA CAPTAINS, SCOUNDRELS AND NUNS

NATIVE ALASKANS

SETTLEMENTS SPRING UP

Archeological evidence suggests that much of Cook Inlet was occupied by Eskimos, who appear to have abandoned the area sometime during historical times. Copper knives, bracelets and beads, as well as metal-cut decorations, have been found around Kachemak Bay.

E A R L Y   A L A S K A

1

UNANSWERED QUESTIONS

After teaching in remote Alaska communities and raising a widower's children, Phyllis Downing Carlson turned her attention to the history of the Great Land. Her quest for knowledge brought her a plethora of questions about Alaska's past, especially regarding the Cook Inlet area.

Why was much of Cook Inlet abandoned by the Eskimos after more than 1,500 years of occupancy? Why and when did the Tanaina Indians move into this territory? Are the cave paintings found in remote sites in Cook Inlet and Kodiak connected with religious and magical practices and who painted them?

Phyllis found some questions answered during her 50-plus-year writing career and did not find answers to others. And sometimes she found that answers brought more questions as she interviewed archaeologists and scholars along the way.

Frederica de Laguna, a dedicated archaeologist who carried out a thorough study of the ancient Eskimo culture in Kachemak Bay during the 1930s, divided the Eskimo period into three stages, which she called Kachemak phases I, II and III. The first she placed at least as far back as 800 B.C., and perhaps further. The last phase appears to continue to historical times and shows evidence of copper knives, bracelets and beads, as well as metal-cut decorations on artifacts.

William Workman, archaeologist and professor of cultural anthropology at the University of Alaska Anchorage, and his wife, Karen,

Some Alaska Eskimos lived in partially underground dwellings called barabaras.

excavated on Yukon Island and found more copper articles. William Workman wrote that there may have been another late pre-historic Eskimo occupancy, and he said there is still "virtually everything to learn about the crucial period in Kachemak Bay pre-history."

And although English Bay and Port Graham still have settlements of Eskimo people, locally known as Aleuts, the answer to why most of the Eskimos left the lower Inlet still puzzles researchers. Were they driven out, did they die out, or, in the process of development, did their elements recede into the background, possibly under Indian influence, as Hans Georg Bandi suggested in his book, "Eskimo Pre-History."

Disputed ownership in Cook Inlet

At any rate, Cook Inlet has been the scene of unsettled and disputed ownership, and during the last decade of the 18th century when the Russians entered the picture, there were midnight raids, ambushes and open warfare, according to historian Hubert Howe Bancroft, author of "History of Alaska, 1730-1885." The Tanaina

Indians of the Kenai Peninsula did not welcome the Russians by any means, and their hostility limited Russian expansion in this part of Alaska.

Why and when did the Tanaina people arrive on the Inlet? That has not been answered, either. The Athabascan nation to which the Tanaina belong stretches through Interior Alaska and Canada. They are connected with the Navajo and Apache by the Na-dene' language.

De Laguna quotes William Healy Dall, 1880 census-taker Ivan Petroff and Baron Wrangell as saying that the Tanaina are relative newcomers to Cook Inlet. Just when the migration took place only can be determined by more archaeological work in the upper Inlet. One ethno-historical study by Joan Townsend places the beginning of Tanaina occupancy around 100 years before the coming of the Russians in the last quarter of the 18th century.

Athabascan Indians make camp in Southcentral Alaska before the turn-of-the-last century. Anthroplogists say there still is virtually everything to learn about Kachemak Bay pre-history.

Earliest reference of Tanaina

When Stepan Glotov, an early Russian fur trader, reached Kodiak in 1762 to trade with the Koniags, a boy told him that they often traded with the Tanainas of Cook Inlet – the earliest reference to the Tanaina. This indicates they were already established before European contact. When Capt. James Cook, in 1778, described the people he met in what is today known as Cook Inlet, they and their culture strongly resembled some late descriptions of the Tanaina.

So the Tanaina were present when the Russians appeared to establish their settlements at Fort Alexander, Fort St. George, Nikolaevsky Redoubt and Fort St. Nicholas, now Kenai. And there was much discontent among the tribes over their treatment by the Russians. Natives of Lake Skilak actively plotted the destruction of all Russians on the Kenai Peninsula. They tried to bridge over the feuds between themselves and the Chugaches, another group of Native Alaskans studied by de Laguna, who lived on the islands and shores of Prince William Sound and along the eastern coast of Kenai Peninsula, and also received encouragement from tribes on the west side of Cook Inlet. It took all of Russian ruler Alexander Baranof's firmness and a liberal distribution of liquor to assert authority over the dissidents.

Natives attack other tribes

Besides fighting the Russians, the Natives also fought among themselves. The Tanaina were frequently at war with the Kodiak Island people and often were attacked by Eskimos from the Prince William Sound area.

It was reported by Natives at Kenai that stones on the Russian River acted as watchmen when the Tanaina were attacked by the Seward region Eskimos.

"These stones belonged to a shaman," the story went. "They were large and had hollows like mouths. When an Eskimo party approached, the first stone hollered loudly and the signal was passed on from stone to stone until it reached the shaman's village. Then the people would hide their belongings in the woods and run away."

Nickafor Alexan, one of the old-timers at the Indian village of

Tyonek on the west side of Cook Inlet, told Aunt Phil of the last Indian war in his village. It was between the Tyonek and Knik people who lived farther north on the Knik Arm. It happened, Alexan said, when the Russians still had their quarters in Kenai.

Last Indian war in Tyonek

The Knik people greatly outnumbered the Tyoneks, so the Knik chief came up with a plot to do away with his enemy. He went up the Yentna River and told the people there that he would pay them well to kill the Tyonek chief. The Knik chief's plan centered around the Yentna people pretending to be Kuskokwim traders when the Tyonek chief and his people went to Merrill Pass, around Mount Spur, to trade with the Kuskokwim people as they did every year.

After being tricked by the Knik people, the tribe of Tyonek concocted a ruse to conquer their enemy. That plan turned into the last Indian war in Tyonek, which is pictured here around 1900.

The Yentna people thoroughly deceived the Tyoneks, Alexan said. As was tradition, there was much singing and dancing. The Yentna people danced in shifts and wore out the visitors, and then they killed all in the Tyonek party except the Tyonek chief's nephew, who got away to tell his tribesmen of the attack.

The survivor told his people that the attackers were really Yentna people. He then led a party up the river and they killed all of the trader-imposters. And while on their avenging raid, the Tyoneks discovered that the Knik chief had been behind the attack, so they vowed revenge on the Knik people, too.

Without betraying his knowledge, the chief's nephew sent word to the Knik people to come down to Tyonek for a potlatch to honor his uncle. When the visitors arrived, they were asked to hand over their weapons as "no trouble was desired." The Tyonek people took the weapons, locked them up and repaid treachery with treachery. All the Knik visitors were killed.

"That," Alexan said, "was the last Indian war in Tyonek."

Tribes around Anchorage

The village of Knik, inhabited by the Knat'a-'na, was near present-day village Eklutna on the east side of Knik Arm near Anchorage. The Cuci'tnat'a settled along the Susitna River and the Tava-na lived at North Forelands and Tyonek. The eastern shore of the Inlet was inhabited by the Yaxt'a-na, whose chief village was Kenai.

There are 20 remembered Kenaitze Indian villages from Point Possession and eastward to Stepanka near Skilak Lake, outlet to Kenai River. Many of the old villages were abandoned as the Indians moved closer to trading posts when the white men came.

Anchorage's Native name was Xatikiuct, as told to de Laguna by Theodore Sasha of Kenai. Around 1880, census-taker Ivan Petroff located a town called "Zdluiat" a little north of the present site of Anchorage, but de Laguna was unable to identify it and thought it might have been the same place where house pits and fortifications have been seen on the north bank of Ship Creek opposite Anchorage.

Tanaina described as least nomadic

Cornelius Osgood, in his "Ethnography of the Tanaina," mentions that the Tanainas were among the least nomadic of the Athabascan people. In the Kenai area, they probably did migrate to get better hunting grounds, but undoubtedly went back to favorite fishing grounds in early spring. In this season, they shared their smokehouses with their drying catch, while in winter, semi-subterranean houses, commonly called barabaras, helped shelter them from the bitter cold.

In the Kachemak region there apparently was sufficient food – probably the only place in the northern Athabascan country where this could be said. The Tanaina were uniquely fortunate because they had sea mammals, fish and land animals, but there was an inequality of food supply inland and in the northern section of the Inlet.

Besides fish, mammals and animals, there were game birds, berries, wild rice, wild peas, onions, fern roots, Kila – parsnip-like plants – and edible seaweed. The Natives made tea from wild rose buds.

Athabascan people of Kenai spent winters in semi-subterranean sod houses called barabaras that sheltered them from the bitter cold.

Herbal remedies and shamans

The Tanaina also used plants as herbal remedies. One kind of western nettle was used for rheumatism. The sufferer was first treated with hot water, and then wrapped with an application of leaves. Roots of colts foot were chewed to stop an appearance of blood in the sputum resulting from consumption tuberculosis. Sage brush was wrapped around cuts and used to break up colds. Red currants were applied to sore eyes.

Shamans might be called upon if herbal remedies did not take care of the situation. Shamans also foretold events and saw what was happening in distant parts as well as healed the sick. Shamans seemed to have acted as advisors, paramedics and medical specialists.

Tyonek's second chief, Sha-E-Dah-Kla, was considered the biggest medicine man in Cook Inlet, according to Alexan.

"Upper Inlet shamans had spirits and wanted to send them to bring sickness to Tyonek, but Sha-E-Dah-Kla caught the bad spirits with his spider net and disappointed them," Alexan said. "The rest of the shamans were scared of Sha-E-Dah-Kla."

Cave paintings

Aunt Phil remembered villagers in Tyonek talking about cave paintings while she taught school there during the 1930s.

"Some of the old-timers told me about them," she later said. "But they're in remote sites and few white people have seen them."

The villagers said some paintings were on Indian Island, Bear Island and Sadie Cove in Kachemak Bay, and in a rock shelter at the head of Tuxedni Bay. Indian tradition says they were made by people who lived there long ago. Cultural deposits point to an antiquity probably greater than that of any known Indian deposits in Kachemak Bay.

Rock paintings have been found at Eskimo sites on Kodiak and Afognak islands, too, where the Athabascans never penetrated in recent migrations from the Interior. In Prince William Sound there are similar paintings that are indisputably Eskimo.

De Laguna believes the Cook Inlet rock paintings are of Eskimo origin, also.

Red hematite, perhaps mixed with animal fat, was used and probably applied with fingers or the frayed end of a stick. The most prominent figure suggests conventionalized symbols used by the Bering Straits Eskimo to depict a raven; men are represented in kayaks and umiaks, two types of Native boats. Sea mammals and land animals are depicted, also, as well as hunting scenes and other activities.

They don't seem to be primarily works of art, as they were not near any permanent villages. Were they painted to secure good luck in hunting and other activities? Were they connected with religious and magical practices of the pre-historical inhabitants of the area?

These types of questions surround carved rocks found in Southeast Alaska, too.

Mouths of salmon streams in Southeast Alaska are filled with inscriptions pecked into hard rock like this one found around Hoonah.

Rock drawings

Alaska's petroglyphs, Greek for rock carving, are among many enigmas of science. Because their true meanings are elusive, they remain a mysterious link to a people who inhabited the world a long time ago.

The carvings are in abundance in Southeastern Alaska and are unique because they are associated with salmon streams, rather than primitive village sites, and always face the sea. Mouths of salmon streams are filled with inscriptions pecked into hard rock like sandstone, slate and granite, while good rocks for carving remain bare in villages near those streams.

To those familiar with the ancient beliefs and oral traditions of the Tlingit and Haida Indians, the petroglyphs show that salmon is life. These Native Alaskans, whose diet was primarily fish, were not hunters and had no agriculture. If the salmon failed to return, it could mean starvation for the clans.

It made sense, therefore, for them to try to avoid small runs and to do everything possible to try and increase the runs. They may have carved images of intermediaries, including deities "Raven" and others in special favor with the Salmon People, on the rocks in an effort to bring salmon back to their communities.

Legend of 'Mouldy End'

Legend has it that a Tlingit boy named Shin-quo-klah, or "Mouldy End," was punished by the Salmon People for wasting dried salmon. They took him under the sea, but they later returned him to his people.

He became a great shaman. It's said that his image is etched on a rock at Karta Bay, placed near where he died after he accidentally killed his own soul, which was inhabited by a supernatural salmon at the time. Copies of the etching were all around the beaches of Hydaburg and Wrangell, where it's believed his influence was being used with the Salmon People to insure adequate runs of salmon.

Petroglyphs also appear in the Kodiak Archipelago, where at least seven sites have carvings that depict human figures, animal forms and geometric designs. There are four large clusters of petroglyphs at Cape Alitak, at the entrance to Alitak Bay. Some Alaskans think that the designs were made to mark territory, to act as permanent signs that linked families with particular subsistence harvesting areas.

The oldest rock drawings appear to have been carved as early as 10,000 years ago, and archaeologists have found similar abstract symbols along the coast of Siberia. There is no way to discern the true intent or motivation of the artists, but the drawings are one of the few sources of ancient art that tie Alaska Natives to their heritage.

Alaska Natives also are tied to their heritage through shamanism.

The Native people of the North designated shamans as their go-betweens with the unknown. Shamans, like the man pictured here with a rope around his neck and kneeling in front of a totem pole, acted as healers and intermediaries with the spirit world.

2

COPING WITH THE UNKNOWN

Every society has its own way of coping with the unknown, and every society has its own way of choosing certain members to act as intermediaries between themselves and the unknown. Many cultures, including the Native people of the North, have designated their go-betweens "shamans."

Siberia, believed by many to be the place where shamanism originated, exported the practices to the North Arctic, and there the shamanistic beliefs found fertile ground. Hartley Burr Alexander, writing in "Mythology of All Races," said:

"In no section of America is the belief in possession by spirits and spiritualistic powers more deeply seated than in the Northwest; shamanism is the key to the whole conception of life which animates myth and rite."

"Kiyesvilavic" is the time when the shamans got busy, which included the months of November through January, the short daylight northern season. Shamanistic contests were held and shamans would pit their prowess against one another. They held séances, spoke with corpses, shook the house, brought in voices of shaman spirits or flew through the air.

Shamans foretell events

Shamans not only served the community by healing the sick, but some of them were able to foretell events and to see what was happening in distant parts. P.E. Goddard tells us in his book, "Indians of the Northwest Coast:"

"Every war party included a shaman, who through his supernatural knowledge, warned of danger and pointed out favorable times for attack. The shaman, by catching or destroying the souls of the enemy, made the killing of their bodies an easy matter."

In healing, the shaman seems to have acted as both paramedic and medical specialist. Two primary causes of illness were recognized by the North Alaskan Eskimo societies — the soul leaving the body, wandering in dreams and failing to return. It wandered, it was believed, because a taboo had been broken and it could not return to its owner. Then, too, there was the concept of intrusion, or the driving of some object into the patient's body by a hostile or malevolent shaman. Another shaman would be required to extract it.

The soul loss was by far the more prevalent cause of illness and the shaman unusually was not immediately called. However, if home remedies would not work, the shaman would be summoned and he first would try to diagnose the illness. If his common sense told him that the patient was beyond curing, witchcraft could be blamed, or a broken restriction that he couldn't handle.

Shamans cure villagers' ills

It is difficult for us to understand some of the cures that were used. R. Spencer, in "North Alaskan Eskimo," tells about one case:

"A shaman could staunch the flow of blood. There was a man at Nuwuk who was making an umiak. He was working with an adz. It slipped and he cut his leg very badly. It was bleeding very much and his wife tried to stop the flow of blood. She was unable to do it. Finally the man sent her to Utkeaayvik for a shaman who was a specialist in such matters.

"She walked down the beach 10 miles or so. Finally she returned with the shaman. The man was weak from the loss of blood and was holding his leg to keep it from bleeding more. The shaman took a drum, sang over the wound and talked over it. When he was done, just a little scratch was left on the skin; there was no wound at all.

Stories passed from generation to generation tell of miracles performed by shamans on their tribesmen. This Yakutat Bay Indian man, wounded in a bear fight, would be a prime candidate for a shaman's healing magic.

They paid him two seal pokes full of oil for his services."

C. Osgood, in "Contributions to the Ethnography of the Kutchin," gave another example:

"There are several men alive today who have been operated upon by shamans. One man had something wrong with his stomach so that the shaman had a special wooden knife made. He opened up the breast of the sufferer and took the end of the esophagus in his mouth and extracted the disease. Then he washed out the stomach and the esophagus snapped back into place. The skin, which had been cut, he folded back and rubbed until it appeared whole, without a trace of a scar. The fact that such stories are numerous, and are accepted without question by the Kutchin, clearly indicates the great influence and power of shamans among these people."

SKA-E-DAH-KLA THE STICK

COPYRIGHT 1906 BY CASE & DRAPER

513

Tyonek's second chief, Sha-E-Dah-Kla, meaning "grandfather of all," was considered the mightiest medicine man in Cook Inlet. He also was called "The Stick."

Shamans were usually men. Although there were some women shamans, they were not considered to have as much power as the men. There were some husband and wife teams, and old men and women often were thought to have developed shaman characteristics.

Sha-E-Dah-Kla: Tyonek's powerful shaman

Tyonek's second chief, Sha-E-Dah-Kla, meaning "grandfather of all," was considered the biggest medicine man in Cook Inlet, according to Nickafor Alexan, who recorded much of the history of the village of Tyonek.

Alexan befriended Aunt Phil during her tenure as a teacher in Tyonek during the 1930s, and he told her about the village shaman, who also was known as "The Stick."

"I understand that this story told to me about medicine men partly will sound incredible, but old people saying it, said it was true," Alexan told her. "Some of the old people telling it to me said they saw it with their own eyes — they have done many miracles in front of people and also cured lots of sick people."

Alexan said he heard that all medicine men around Cook Inlet were afraid of Sha-E-Dah-Kla, because he had more power in his spirit than most shamans. According to legend, he had a spider net outside of North Foreland with his spirit. Because the upper shamans had bad spirits and wanted to send their bad spirits to bring bad sickness to Tyonek, Sha-E-Dah-Kla caught the bad spirits with his spider net and disappointed them.

"That is why those shamans were scared of him," Alexan said. "[At the] same time, when this Sha-E-Dah-Kla became chief of Tyonek, he went up to the Kuskokwim people and traded with them. Since old grandpa used to trade with them, he made much success and became rich and built a store, bought furs, which he took to Kenai and sold for a high price. He helped many old, poor ladies, as well as old blind men."

Shaman searches for son

One day, one of his sons, named Pete, was playing with other boys his age, about 10 or 12, when he slipped and fell in the creek, Alexan said. The other boys couldn't save him and he drowned.

It was two or three hours before his parents learned about the accident, and by the time they arrived at the creek, it was high tide and the creek was full of water. Sha-E-Dah-Kla came down to where his son drowned, but he couldn't see to the bottom because the water was muddy.

"Sha-E-Dah-Kla went to dive in and look for him, but his wife and the others didn't want him to as they thought he would drown, too," Alexan said.

So the shaman told them to tie rawhide string around his waist tight, and tie a stick on other end. He said they should follow him wherever that stick traveled.

He then dove into the water and went up the river first, but the tide was coming in about 100 yards up, so he turned around.

"He never came back," Alexan said. "But they knew by the stick [he was still in the water], so they kept on following that wherever it goes. And then he was going down the river, until almost down to the mouth of the creek. By the way the stick was floating back and forth across the creek, they knew he was searching. Finally he came up with the body across his arms."

Sha-E-Dah-Kla saves his son

Alexan said the mighty shaman came ashore, carried his son's body up to their house and laid his body down.

"He said he would go after his son's spirit and bring him back, so he lay by his dead son, and they were both covered with a blanket," Alexan said. "After a while, his wife felt his heart — he, too, was dead. He had told them not to bother him when he laid by his son, which was early in the evening.

"Not until early in the morning did his wife feel for their hearts, because she was afraid and thought they would never come back to life again."

But fortunately the son began warming up, and then after about half an hour, his father started warming up. Then the son's pulse began to beat. Soon his father's pulse started to beat.

"And then he woke up. So they came to life again," Alexan said. "Some miracle. As I see this man, Pete, I notice his eyes look like sleepy eyes."

Alexan told Aunt Phil that another unbelievable miracle happened to Sha-E-Dah-Kla, too. While he was sleeping in the smokehouse, which many people did because mosquitoes were thick in the region, the ridge pole on which dried fish hung broke. The resulting crash scared the shaman spirit out of him.

"After that he was kind of weak and forgot all about his shaman work," Alexan said. "His spirit went up in the air and drifted down somewhere, I hear down to the Aleut country."

Shaman spirit leaves Sha-E-Dah-Kla

"When I was a small boy, they used to tell us children not to holler in the evening, because if these spirits are drifting around, they always come down where there is hollering," Alexan said. "Whenever this spirit landed, that village got some sickness — it would come out sometimes and kill lots of people if other shamans don't find it. Sometimes, I hear, some bad shaman sent their spirits to kill people — then they would have to destroy it."

However, if the spirit said it just got lost and didn't know where its home was, Alexan explained, other shamans would show it which way to go and send it back.

Which is what happened to Sha-E-Dah-Kla's spirit when it got lost and landed in an Aleut village, according to Alexan. A strong shaman caught it, asked it lots of questions and sent the lost spirit home.

"When a spirit is sent home, it has more power than it took with it, because it also takes with it what the other shaman worked with to get a hold of it to ask it questions," Alexan said. "I understand that when Chief Sha-E-Dah-Kla's spirit came back to him, the spirit was too big for his body. That time the spirit busted up the legs and arms (of the Native chief)."

In such a case, the injured shaman is put outside in the evening where no one comes around. Usually the shaman's spirit heals the physical body and the shaman will come to life again by morning.

Shaman heals

"They put Chief Sha-E-Dah-Kla's body out, and when his wife thought he was about healed up in the morning at daylight, she came out to see," Alexan said. "But no, not quite."

The chief's legs were not quite healed, but after another evening, he came to life again with all his limbs working properly. His family took him back inside their house, where he sang shaman songs and worked on himself until he really got well.

"Some miracle!" Alexan said. "I understand he used that medicine for good causes only and cured lots of people with it. After his two sons were grown up, he got sick and died. I think a big strong shaman could die, too. As well as the best doctors could die in this world. ..."

While many people might view these stories as pure fantasy, and think such events could not have happened, researchers say it's a question of spirituality.

"Shamanism in its modern aspect is neither a science, a religion nor a philosophy," wrote Rick A. Morris in his paper, "Shamanism, Common Sense and Parapsychology." "It is spiritualistic ... its study more properly relegated to parapsychology ... a field capable of viewing the incredulous with credulity."

3

ISLAND OF MYSTERY

Capt. James Cook reported seeing a tall, sail-like rock about 60 miles west of Dutch Harbor in 1778. Unbeknownst to him and his crew, a 6,000-foot volcano lay beneath the conical mountain and its crater sat just below sea level.

At various times throughout Alaska's history, navigators' logs recorded changes in the volcanic island's shoreline from season to season. Sometimes it was said to have disappeared into the ocean, only to emerge later in other locations.

The mystery island, named Bogoslof, is composed of black sand that's unstable and shifts with the tide. Its first recorded eruption occurred in the mid-1790s.

Early in May 1796, amid thunder, earthquake and steam, the volcanic island, later called Castle Rock, emerged from the depths of the sea. Otto von Kotzebue, an early Russian explorer, was told about it by Kriukof, a resident agent of the Russian-American Company at Unalaska. Kriukof, along with Native Aleuts of Umnak and Unalaska, saw the birth of the island because they were on the northernmost part of Umnak Island when the cataclysm occurred.

Island rises from the sea

According to Kriukof, on May 7 a storm came in from the north-west and a terrific roaring came back from mountains to the south. An island could be seen rising from the foaming waters, and amid the shaking of the earth, stones were cast from it as far as Umnak, 30

Capt. James Cook reported seeing Bogoslof, left, in the Aleutians in 1778. Castle Rock, center, rose amid thunder, earthquake and steam in 1796, and Fire Island, right, poked through the water's surface in 1883.

miles away. At sunrise the earth stopped shaking, flames diminished and the newly risen island, shaped like a black cap, could be seen.

The island grew in height and circumference, and smoke and steam continued to pour forth. Even after eight years, Natives reported the water around the island was warm and the ground was so hot no one could walk on it.

The Aleuts called the new island Agashagok, but since it had appeared on St. John's Day in their calendar, the Russians called it Joanna Bogoslova, for St. John the Theologian.

Bogoslof continued to change throughout the years, and the Aleutians continued to shake. Another peak estimated at 800 feet high heaved up about a mile north of the first peak in 1883. It was called Fire Island. Deep water separated these two peaks at first, but land later formed between them. In 1884, Lt. Stoney, visiting the area on the ship *Corwin*, stated that many earthquake shocks could be felt even onboard the anchored schooner.

More islands form

Another eruption in 1906 brought up two more peaks, each about 400 feet tall. Within a year, these two peaks disappeared after the washing by icy waters and winds wore them down. As late as 1910 violent shocks hit Dutch Harbor, shocks probably associated with formation of new islands in the Bogoslof group.

Lt. George E. Morris Jr. led a team to chart the island in the mid-1930s. After 10 weeks of surveying, Morris noted that the island's reputation for shifting position and changing in appearance could be accounted for by reasons other than faulty navigation.

"Without doubt there were changes in the contours of the island only after each eruption," he wrote in his journal. "Although the island is small, it presents a marked difference in appearance when viewed from different directions. Anyone seeing the island from one direction at one time and from another direction at a later time might believe the island had changed even though there had been no eruption."

Mysterious island is home to sea lions and birds

Morris also discovered the volcanic island teeming with sea lions that used it as a breeding place. He found hundreds of them on the beach during June and July.

"The continuous roar and barking of the herd made a noise like an airplane at close quarters," he noted. "The herd was quiet for only a few of the very early hours of the morning."

While charting the island, Morris also found that sea gulls, murres and a few other species of birds were "the only other inhabitants of the island besides ourselves and the sea lions."

"About 1,000 gulls were nesting on the plateau ... they lay two or three eggs in the nest about the first of June ... The pallas murres arrived between the first and fifteenth of June. There were soon 50,000 of them, by conservative estimate, nesting on pinnacle rocks and Castle Rock."

The surveying team eventually determined that the charted positions of the shoreline of Unalaska and Umnak islands were in error by a few miles, which probably accounted for the impression that Bogoslof changed its position from time to time.

Explorers around Bogoslof Island in the Bering Sea reported seeing an abundance of sea lions, pictured here in July 1899. Lt. George E. Morris Jr. also found the island teeming with the noisy mammals in 1930.

4

Earthquakes Form Landscape

Along with Bogoslof and the Aleutian Islands, the story of Alaska's earthquake history has been written on other parts of its landscape, too – its riverbeds, glaciers and mountains – in the centuries before and since man set foot on the Great Land.

Most of the early earthquake accounts are fragmentary. There are mentions of two in the Aleutians and the Alaska Peninsula as early as 1786 and 1788, when "the land was overflowed by a sea wave, and some lives were lost."

Far from Bogoslof and the Aleutians is Sitka in Southeastern Alaska, another section of Alaska that has had more than its share of ups and downs. The giant earthquake that rattled Southeast in July 1972 was the most severe shaker since the Good Friday quake in 1964; buildings swayed, pictures fell from the walls and cars bounced on city streets where the strongest shocks were felt.

But on April 2, 1836, the whole coast of Southeast Alaska shook when an earthquake triggered a series of waves that threatened to wipe out the entire town of Sitka. It happened near the Feast of the Annunciation.

Bishop Ivan Veniaminov was in charge of the Russian Orthodox Church, St. Michael's Cathedral, in Sitka on April 2, 1836, when an earthquake triggered a series of waves that threatened to wipe out the entire town.

Survivors give thanks

Bishop Ivan Veniaminov, in charge of the Russian Church at the time and who became known as St. Innocent, ordained, that in order to give thanks for the town's salvation, a procession should march through all of Sitka's streets – not only on that year, but each year thereafter on this church holiday.

The procession marched around the town and blessed all the thoroughfares with holy water. This annual Annunciation Day procession was discontinued sometime after 1900.

But Sitka has continued to have quakes; a severe one in 1917, and again in 1927, caused all of Southeastern Alaska to shake. The clocks stopped and cracks appeared in buildings.

To give thanks for their salvation from the April 1836 earthquake, Bishop Ivan Veniaminov ordained that a procession should march through Sitka's streets every year on Annunciation Day.

Another part of Alaska that has suffered much from earthquakes is around Yakutat Bay. On Sept. 3, 1899, and again on Sept. 10, that area was sent into great upheaval. The earthquakes were widely felt, but since there were no villages in the vicinity, the 30-foot wave that hit land did little damage and only a few Natives and prospectors were eyewitnesses. Important topography changes took place, however, and evidence of the damage is unmistakable.

Vertical displacement evidence

The U.S. Geological party that went into the region six years later found dead barnacles and other shellfish strewn everywhere and beaches raised 17 feet or more over a considerable area. The vertical displacement of the 1899 quake is said to be the largest studied up to that point. Clam borings and barnacles were reported to have been lifted as much as 47 feet above the sea and other areas were depressed.

Coastal glaciations were affected by the quake, too. Many glaciers in the St. Elias Range became active and advanced hundreds of yards in less than a year. A few glaciers reacted differently and began an abnormally fast retreat. In some cases, greatly crevassed glacier fronts were found six years later, showing that it had taken that length of time for the fractured area to reach the sea.

If the 30-some-foot wave did no damage at Yakutat in 1899, Lituya Bay, 80 miles away, had an earthquake in 1936 that triggered an enormous wave that spread debris over the ocean for 50 miles. But that was just a curtain raiser to the main event.

Giant wave in Lituya Bay

On a fine June evening in 1958, all hell broke lose at Yakutat and Lituya Bay. At about 10:17 p.m. an earthquake began to shake a vast area of Southeastern Alaska and northern British Columbia. At Yakutat, five people had been picking strawberries on an island in the bay. Two left in their boat just before the quake, but the portion of the island where the other three were standing heaved 20 feet into the air, then sank beneath the water. There were no signs of the missing trio except a few picnic plates floating on the surface. The water is said to be 200 feet deep now at the point.

Although Lituya Bay may not have been the center of the shock, it suffered the greatest devastation.

"The mountains were shaking something awful, with slides of rocks and snow," said one eyewitness on a fishing boat in the area. "But what I noticed mostly was the glacier, the north one they call Lituya Glacier.

"I know you can't ordinarily see that glacier from where I was anchored, and people shake their heads when I tell them I saw it that night. I can't help it if they don't believe me. I know the glacier is hidden by the point when you are in the cove, but I know what I saw that night, too."

An earthquake in Southeast Alaska in 1958 caused a tidal wave of mammoth proportions in Lituya Bay, pictured here in 1948.

Unbelievable sight

"The glacier had risen in the air and moved forward so it was in sight," the eyewitness recounted. "It must have risen several hundred feet. I don't mean it was just hanging in the air. It seemed to be solid, but it was jumping and shaking like crazy. Big chunks of ice were falling off the face of it and down into the water … suddenly the glacier dropped back out of sight and there was a big wall of water going over the point."

A geologist who studied the area doesn't shake his head in disbelief at the story.

"It's perfectly plausible. The glacier lies right on the fault line and almost anything could have happened," the geologist said.

At Lituya Bay there is a great "loose joint" in the earth's crust, the geologist said. Some of the world's mightiest peaks and glaciers lie astride it, and when earthquakes occur, mountains twist, shake and tumble around; uplift and subsidence that accompanied the Good Friday earthquake in 1964 affected an area of at least 34,000 square miles, with western coastal land levels rising as much as 7.5 feet, and to the west the land level subsided as much as 5.4 feet.

Yes, the story of Alaska's earthquakes is written in our landscape. The evidence attests to Nature's awesome power. Nature has always seemed to mock man's puny efforts to tame her. So far, however, she hasn't succeeded in shaking us off.

The Good Friday earthquake in March 1964 caused heavy damage in the port city of Seward and the tidal wave that followed devastated much of the area.

TIME OF DISCOVERY

5

WHILE THE UNITED STATES WAS BEING BORN

While the First Continental Congress presented its Declaration of Rights and Grievances to King George III in 1774, Spaniard Juan Perez had been ordered by his government to explore the west coast of America to latitude 60 degrees, "but not to disturb the Russians."

The Russians were already in Alaska. Emilian Bassov, a sergeant of the military company of lower Kamchatka, and Andrei Serebrennikov, a merchant from Moscow, had formed a partnership in 1743 to hunt for sea otter along the Aleutian Chain. In 1745, more Russians were landing at Agati and Attu. By 1758, the year before Maj. Gen. James Wolfe captured Quebec, a Turinsk merchant named Stepan Glottof had made it

Russians Emilian Bassov and Andrei Serebrennikov formed a partnership in 1743 to hunt for sea otter along the Aleutian Chain. Shortly thereafter, Russians were trading with the Aleuts in the area.

as far as Umnak and Unalaska in search of fur and was peacefully trading with the Aleuts there.

By 1763, the year that King George III prohibited colonists from settling west of the Appalachian Mountains, Glottof had reached Kodiak, running into stiff fighting from the fierce Koniags. And about the time the colonists were writhing under the Stamp and the Townsend acts levying duties on paper, glass, paint and tea, the Russian brigantine *Chichagof* was planning to explore Bering Straits.

Revolutionary war vs. exploration

The Boston Tea Party occurred the year before Perez sailed on his voyage of exploration. He managed to escape confrontation with the Russians, for his voyage was far to the south of theirs. In 1775, when the battle of Lexington and Concord started the Revolutionary War, Perez, along with Bruno Heceta and Juan Francisco de Bodega y Cuadra, was discovering Mount Edgecumbe and Shelikof Bay.

In 1776, while the Second Continental Congress was adopting the Declaration of Independence, orders were issued by the Spanish to outfit another expedition to continue and complete the discoveries of Perez, although it wasn't until 1779 that the expedition finally set sail.

Another, more famous, explorer started out in 1776, too. Just eight days after the signing of the Declaration of Independence, Capt. James Cook sailed from England on his epic voyage. As he lay at anchor in Portsmouth harbor at the beginning of his voyage, three transports also were getting ready to sail, loaded with English and Hessian troops to suppress the American rebels. Cook's vessels, however, were exempt from capture by the enemy by special convention because of the international benefits expected from his expedition to discover the Northwest Passage.

Valley Forge vs. fur trading

The year 1776 also saw the Russian Shelikof forming a fur-hunting partnership with Lebedef-Lashtochkin, foretelling the establishment of the Russian-American Company. And in the winter of 1777-1778, while George Washington was holding his army together at Valley Forge, Shelikof and his partners were busy on fur-trading expeditions. During the crucial years of the Revolutionary War, Shelikof was outfitting a vessel for the Aleutian fur trade in pursuit of the precious sea otter.

Cook sailed out of Nooka Bay in 1778, exploring the Alaska coast as far north as Norton Sound. Another famous name in exploration was heard of about that time, too, for George Rogers Clark was leading a force down the Ohio River, winning a series of victories on the way.

In 1779, the Spanish, commanded by Ignacio Arteaga and accompanied by Cuadra, were exploring around the Copper River country and the entrance to Cook Inlet. When they sighted the Iliamna Volcano, they named it "Miranda."

Capt. James Cook sailed out of Nooka Bay in 1778, exploring the Alaska coast as far as Norton Sound.

During the stirring years of the Revolution, knowledge of the North Country was being gathered by English and other European explorers, as well as Russian fur gatherers. While the Philadelphia Convention was drawing up the Constitution that was later ratified by all 13 states, "Englishmen under the English flag, Englishmen under the Portuguese flag, Spanish and Russians were cruising around, often within a few miles of one another, taking possession for one nation or the other of all the lands in sight," in Alaska, according to Hubert Howe Bancroft in "History of Alaska, 1730-1885."

Colonization ending vs. colonization beginning

The fame of the new fur country spread; on the coastline stretching from California to the Aleutians, the Spanish were in the southeast, the Russians in the northwest and in between lay thousands of miles of no-man's land claimed by Russians, English and Spanish.

Just as a new epoch of American history began with the defeat of the English at Yorktown and the attempt at unification of the 13 colonies through the Articles of Confederation, a new epoch was beginning in Alaska, too. In 1783 Shelikof sailed from Okhotsk to establish a base for colonization in Russian America. In 1788 an imperial edict gave this company exclusive rights over the region.

One year after George Washington was elected the first President of the new United States, Alexander Andreevich Baranof sailed from Okhotsk to become the first manager of the Russian-American Company. He reached All Saints Bay on Kodiak the year the first 10 amendments – the Bill of Rights – were ratified.

Alexander Andreevich Baranof sailed from Okhotsk to become the first manager of the Russian-American Company in the mid-1780s.

So while the United States was struggling to become a nation after throwing off the yoke of colonialism, Alaska, which later became its northernmost state, was being explored, exploited and taken over by western nations. Its colonization was beginning just about the time the colonization of the United States was coming to an end.

6

NATIVES ATTACK RUSSIAN FORTS

After finding a spot about six miles north of the present town of Sitka, Alexander Baranof exchanged beads and other trading goods for a small piece of Tlingit ground on which to erect a Russian settlement in 1800.

Although the inhabitants of the new trading post became less fearful of an attack from their Tlingit neighbors during the next two years, the Natives in the area remained sullen and hostile toward the Russian intruders. By 1802, they were ready to take back their land.

Old Russian Trading Post, Sitka, Alaska.

E. W. Merrill, Photographer

Tlingit Indians climbed over the stockade and massacred the Russian men in the settlement at the trading post at Sitka in 1802.

Sitka was originally inhabited by a major Tlingit tribe that called the village "Shee Atika." Russian explorer Vitus Bering arrived with his expedition in 1741, and in 1804, Alexander Baranof named the site New Archangel.

That summer, while Baranof was away in Kodiak, a horde of warriors quietly crept out of the woods and climbed over the stockade at Mikhailovsk before any alarm was made.

The Russians attempted to barricade the main buildings, but the assailants broke down the doors and windows and poured into the settlement.

A hunter, who survived the massacre and destruction of the fort, later told his tale.

Hunter tells of attack

"In this present year 1802, about the 24th of June – I do not remember the exact date, but it was a holiday – about two o'clock in the afternoon, I went to the river to look for our calves, as I had been detailed by the commander of the fort, Vassili Medvednikof, to take care of the cattle," the hunter said.

"On returning soon after, I noticed at the fort a great multitude of Kolosh people, who had not only surrounded the barracks below, but were already climbing over the balcony and to the roof with guns and cannon; and standing upon a little knoll in front of the outhouses, was the Sitka toyon, or chief, Mikhail, giving orders to those who were around the barracks, and shouting to some people in canoes not far away, to make haste and assist in the fight."

The Tlingits soon slaughtered the men within the settlement and carried the women and children away as slaves. After emptying out the buildings, they set fire to the compound and retreated back into the woods and their villages.

The hunter spent eight days hiding in the woods, until he spotted an English ship in the bay and then told its commander his story.

Baranof rebuilds fort

Capt. Barber accompanied the hunter to the destroyed fort, where they examined and buried the dead. He then seized the Tlingit chiefs and threatened to hang them if they did not hand over all captives and possessions taken from the Russian post.

The commander took the returned survivors to Kodiak, where he demanded Baranof pay him 50,000 rubles in furs as ransom. Baranof, learning that the captain's only expense had been in feeding and clothing his passengers, paid him 10,000 rubles for the release of three Russians, five Aleut men and 18 women and children.

In April 1804, Baranof returned to Sitka with four small ships, 300 canoes, and a crew of 121 Russians and 800 Aleuts. He retook the fort, erected a stronger stockade and buildings and renamed the settlement New Archangel.

Nulato fort destroyed

The Koyukuk region came to the attention of the rest of the country, too, when in 1851, Koyukon Natives destroyed the Russian fort at Nulato.

Nulato, an Athabascan village on the Yukon River, became a trading center for the Russians when Russian-American Company assistant navigator Petr Malakhov, a Creole, traveled from the company's western fur depot in St. Michael up the Yukon River and arrived in the fish camp town around 1839. When he entered the mouth of the Koyukuk, he gave it the name of Kuyukuk, the word for "river" in the coastal language of the Chnagmyut.

Malakhov saw Nulato's trading potential when he observed coastal Eskimos come to the village offering seal and whale oil, tobacco and copper spearheads in trade. He noticed the spearheads bore the imprint of a forge in Irkutsk, which indicated the visiting Eskimos bartered with Chukchi Natives.

The villagers welcomed trade with the Russians and sent Malakhov back to St. Michael with 350 beaver pelts. Although the company sent no other explorers, traders routinely traveled the rivers to collect furs and the Russian Orthodox Church sent priests all over the area.

For 12 years, the Russians traded peacefully with the village of Nulato, which means "dog salmon camp." But on a dark Sunday, Feb. 16, 1851, that all changed when the Koyukon Indians came to town.

The Koyukon Athabascans traditionally had spring, summer, fall and winter camps and moved as the wild game migrated. They had about a dozen fish camps on the Yukon River between the Koyukuk and the Nowitna rivers. Nulato was the trading site between the Koyukon and the Inupiat Eskimos from the Kobuk area, but western contact increased rapidly after the Russians penetrated the country.

Marauding Koyukuk Indians attack

Another Russian fur trader named Darabin, who reportedly drank heavily, built himself a fortified trading post in Nulato to protect his goods, himself and his private stock. On the day of the massacre, he was entertaining about a dozen British seamen, led by naval officer Lt. Barnard, who were searching for any survivors of famous explorer Sir John Franklin's lost expedition of 1845-47.

A marauding band of Koyukuk Indians from farther upriver, some said led by fanatical shaman Red Shirt, crept into the village and stuffed bundles of grass in the trading post's chimney to smoke out the Russian trader. The men fled the smoke-filled post, only to find arrows flying in their direction.

One arrow killed Darabin, and others found their marks in the seamen. Some sources say that a few seamen escaped and made it back to their ship, the *HMS Enterprise*, while others report that all were picked off as they fled the log building.

The Koyukuk warriors killed all the people in the village, except a small boy and girl who hid underneath canoes pulled ashore and

Famous medicine man Red Shirt was implicated in the massacre at Nulato in 1851.

stored in the snow. The children had fled to the woods when the marauders set fire to the village and told their stories decades later.

The only other survivors were several hunters who'd gone north in search of moose and had left the village with fewer men than usual. One can only imagine the horror that met their eyes when they returned.

Many theories have arisen to explain the massacre, including Russian oppression and brutal treatment of the Indians, rivalries between shamans, the peremptory tone of Lt. Bernard when addressing the Koyukuk chief, or perhaps a dispute over local trade.

The Russian-American Company established a fur depot in St. Michael and collected furs from Natives and traders up the Yukon River.

Shaman travels with explorers

Lt. Lavrentii A. Zagoskin, a special explorer of the Russian-American Company, traveled around the area eight years before the Nulato massacre. In his book, "Lieutenant Zagoskin's Travels in Russian American, 1842-1844," he wrote about the Nulato post and his ethnographic and geographic investigations in the Yukon and Kuskokwim valleys.

With his party that traveled up the Yunnaka, as he called the Koyukuk, was a shaman who had been invited to cure a sick person in a village along the river. The villagers were afraid of catching small-pox from the Russians, and the shaman, Otezokat (Lone Walker), purified their route by setting fires along the trail.

Zagoskin reconnoitered part of the crossing to Kotzebue Sound, which convinced him that real communication existed between the Natives of the Yukon and Koyukuk and the Eskimos living along Kotzebue Sound.

Traders on the Koyukuk

Jimmy Huntington, whose grandfather was a Native trader, wrote about the trading process in his book, "On the Edge of Nowhere."

"All year he (Huntington's grandfather) traded among his own people. Then with the first long days of March, he would make his way down the Hogatza to the head of the Dakli River, the divide between Eskimo and Indian lands, and there he would meet Schilikuk, the Eskimo trader. This was permitted because each need-ed things that only the other had, and it was the only known peaceful contact between the two races ... the Dakli was a five-day trek for a good, strong dog team, and on the other side, the Eskimo would be making his way south along the Selawik River, and the great trading ritual began.

"First, the old Native man would walk, alone and unarmed, to the top of the divide. He carried only a long pole. If he saw no sign of the Eskimo trader, he would stick his pole straight up in the snow and return to camp. Every day it wasn't storming, he walked back up the long hill, looking to see if a second pole had been stuck in the snow alongside his. That was the sign that Schilikuk had arrived, and that trading would begin the next good day."

Trading ritual

"Everything would be laid out in the snow ... there were tanned hides and wolverine fur for parka ruffs. There was a mound of soft, red rock, found only along the Koyukuk, which could be dipped in

Eskimos hunted for seal and sometimes traded the skins for red rock from the Koyukuk region.

water and used to paint snowshoes a brilliant red.

"Meanwhile, the Eskimo was laying out his stuff, too — salt from the Bering Sea and sealskins to make mukluks. Making believe they couldn't care less, the two traders would then inspect each other's goods. Say, the Eskimo wanted a handful of red rock. He would pick it up; walk over to his own pile of things and toss a sealskin off to the side — that meant that he was offering to pay that much for the rock.

"If my grandfather wasn't satisfied, and of course it was part of the ritual that he had to pretend to be insulted by the first offer — he would pull a second skin out of the Eskimo's pile, and that was Schilikuk's signal to look hurt. He'd snatch back both skins, and they would have to start all over again. ..."

Traders in another part of the Great Land came up with an ingenious idea to unload another common Alaska commodity to the folks who lived "Outside." And it didn't involve furs or rocks.

7

WOODY ISLAND'S ICY PAST

A little "two-by-four" island a couple of miles off the city of Kodiak has a number of Alaska's firsts. The first horses in Alaska were brought here, the first road was constructed, the first iron rails were put in and the first field of oats was sown. And they were all put in place to support one thing: a sawmill, so the residents could start what many people called "Alaska's Wackiest Industry" – selling ice.

The sawmill established on Woody Island was perhaps unique in commercial enterprises because its main product was sawdust, which was needed to preserve ice – something abundant in Alaska that California wanted.

In 1851, Californians were in the midst of a gold boom and could afford such luxuries as ice to chill their drinks and keep their food from spoiling. But ice sent from Boston via Cape Horn was very expensive and not enough could be supplied to meet the demand. Alaska was closer. The first shipment of ice was sent from Sitka in February 1852, and it sold for about $75 a ton in San Francisco.

Some authorities contend that the secret and principal object of the American Russian Commercial Company, or the "Ice Company," as it was generally called, was not to deal in ice. They say it was to supply Alaska with provisions during the Crimean War when it was feared that Alaska might fall into British hands. But it's beside the

Woody Island residents built a sawmill, similar to this one in Copper Center, to make sawdust to insulate ice before they sent it via steamship to rich Californians after the Gold Rush of 1848.

point whether the "ice business" was just a blind. It proved profitable, after an uncertain start, and provided work and profits for many years.

Woody Island ice predictable

Little Woody Island profited, too, for ice from Sitka proved unpredictable due to that city's mild climate. Once – in the winter of 1853-54 – a California ice ship had to chip ice from Baird Glacier because Sitka had no ice that winter.

The first mention of the ice establishment on Woody Island comes in 1855 in a letter from Lt. Doroshin to Gen. Helmerson, according to "Seal and Salmon Fisheries and General Resources of Alaska IV."

"On Wood Island, Kodiak Harbor, during a number of years past, horses have been kept to perform certain labor in connection with a mysterious ice company and for the use of these horses a field of 12 acres of oats is regularly sown."

The ice company encountered some financial trouble in 1859, and a Capt. Furuhelm was sent to put matters on a better footing; a new contract was arranged and the depot of the American Russian Commercial Company was fixed on Woody Island.

Before this, two large ice houses were built on Woody Island during 1852-53, when it was discovered that 40-acre Lake Tanignak could supply better ice than Sitka. To keep the ice from melting, a water-powered mill was erected to produce sawdust in which to pack the ice until it was shipped.

Between 1852 and 1859, more than 7,000 tons of ice was shipped as far south as Mexico and Central and South America, bringing at first $75 a ton. Later, the price fell to $7 a ton as the quantity increased.

Ice farce fostered

A farce almost unequalled in history occurred during this time, as well, according to Yule Chaffin, author of "From Koniag to King Crab." An artificial ice machine was invented in the early 1850s, but the machines were expensive and few people could afford them.

No. 5. 20 TON ICE MACHINE.

Ice machines, similar to this New York and St. Clair machine, were invented in the mid-1850s. An ice machine manufacturing company offered to pay the Alaska ice company on Woody Island not to ship ice to California so it could get a foothold in the market.

In order to stifle competition, the ice machine manufacturer offered to pay a set sum every year to the Alaska ice company not to ship the ice it chipped out of Lake Tanignak.

The contract between them was renewed for a number of years, and in order to make sure the ice machine manufacturers wouldn't back out of the agreement, Woody Island residents continued to put up new ice each year, letting the old ice melt. An article by Jay Stauter in the January 1956 Alaska Sportsman magazine called it "Alaska's Wackiest Enterprise" – a sawmill that sawed lumber to make sawdust to preserve ice that was thrown away to make room for a freshly cut supply of ice that never would be used.

A crew of between 150 and 200 Natives were kept busy in winter cutting and storing the ice. In summer they hunted sea otter. A description of life on Woody Island at that time was written by

Some ice company workers lived in simple wooden structures, like this one pictured along the shores of Woody Island in 1915.

Nicholas Pavlof, whose father had been lieutenant governor under Prince Matsoutoff in 1858.

A day in the life of ice workers

"Winter work hours were from 8-11 a.m. and from noon to 4-5 p.m., if the weather was clear. At noon, each man got his half-chark (a wine glass) full of rum and a four-quart iron pot of fish soup made from salt salmon, potatoes and graham flour ... in the evening another half chark of rum and 20 cents as pay for the day's work.

"When the men were brought to their new habitation, there was a meeting among them and they elected a tione (chief) of a highest clan, a practical man in hunting, etc.; they then elected a sacaschik (second chief) who was to go with the hunting parties.

"In 1867, after the transfer, the tione, sacaschik and half a dozen 'wise men' were called to assemble at the agent's house and the agent told them that this company intended to continue the ice business and give them work and assistance; that they would treat them right; that the day's pay would be 40 cents instead of 20; that they will have fish soup week days and salt beef soup on Sundays and two half-charks of rum a day; that they will be furnished with fresh salmon, when possible to obtain them, and dried salmon, whale oil and kimack for winter rations at each week's end, and in case of sickness, they will be attended to. ..."

A view of the settlement

In an article in the Overland Monthly of June 1872, E.L. Keithahn described the Woody Island establishment:

"... their houses are not so well built as those of their neighbors', being merely large holes in the ground, covered with a roof of timber. The church, recently erected by the Company, has a bell and is crowded with Natives every Sunday. At noon, when the bell strikes, the workmen, all warmly clad in European costume, flock from all quarters for their ration of vodka, or black rum ... these men are small of stature, strongly built, and bowlegged from their cramped position while occupying the bidarkas."

According to the 1880 Census, 156 people lived in 13 frame and log houses and eight barabaras on Woody Island. They were engaged in sea otter hunting during the summer and cutting up and storing ice during the winter. A small shipyard was there, too, where little vessels of 25 to 30 tons were built for fishing and trade.

The life of the company manager seems to have been envied by many writers and visitors of the period.

"He had a comfortable home, good food and not much to do but enjoy life during the summer months," according to Chaffin. "A road around the island had been built, the first in Alaska, to exercise a stable of horses imported from Russia. They were the first horses in Alaska and used in winter to haul ice to the storage sheds. For many years they were the only ones in the territory."

Ice business figured into purchase of Alaska

The story of the ice industry covers a span of about 20 years, during both the Russian and American administrations. An interesting footnote to the acquisition of Alaska and the payment thereof is a theory proposed by Keithahn in "Alaska Ice Inc." Keithahn writes that the ice company figured in Alaska's sale price of $7.2 million.

"… perhaps it was for its nuisance value only, but at any rate, the American Russian Commercial Company figured in the purchase of Alaska and accounted for approximately three percent of the entire price paid."

The end of the ice industry came when the Southern Pacific Railroad was built to the coast, making it feasible to ship natural ice from the Sierras into San Francisco, and when artificial ice was invented the price was forced too low to justify Alaska expenses. The ice venture finally folded, but it demonstrated, according to Keithahn, "the ice in 'Seward's ice box' could be turned to a pretty profit!"

Secretary of State Seward did, indeed, foresee a profit in the vast land called Alaska. He was interested in purchasing the territory from the Russians as far back as the 1850s, but he had to wait until after the American Civil War for his dream to become a reality.

8

LAST SHOT OF CIVIL WAR

Two years before the United States purchased Alaska, and almost two months after the Confederate Army stopped fighting on land, the last gun of the Civil War was fired in the Bering Sea.

Not knowing the war had ended in Appomattox 74 days earlier, the commander of an English-built Confederate vessel named *The Shenandoah* fired upon several whalers near St. Lawrence Island on June 22, 1865. Vessels flying British, French and Hawaiian flags were inspected and let pass, but American whalers were seized, according to an article written by Robert N. DeArmond in the July 1937 issue of The Alaska Sportsman.

The Shenandoah was one of several ships used by the Confederates to disrupt Yankee commerce on the high seas. The 1,100-ton steamer was built in Glasgow in 1863 and purchased by the Confederate government in 1864. She measured 230 feet, had a 32-foot beam and drew 15 feet of water.

During her 13-month saga with the Confederate Navy, *The Shenandoah* covered 58,000 miles and captured 38 Yankee ships, including 25 after the war was over. And her crew never took a life.

Following the capture of the American whalers in the Bering Sea, *The Shenandoah* followed other whalers that had slipped into the Arctic Ocean. She passed through the Bering Strait and into the Arctic, but after a few miles, was forced to turn southward due to ice.

While sailing in a dense fog, *The Shenandoah* slammed into ice floes that almost tore off her rudder and threatened to crush her hull. After several hours, however, she managed to steam free of the ice and continue on her course.

The Shenandoah sailed down the Aleutian Chain and set a course for the coast of California. On Aug. 2, just 13 days out of San Francisco, she overtook the English bark *Barracouta*. That's when the crew learned the war was over.

The last gun of the Civil War was shot from *The Shenandoah* on June 22, 1865, when its Confederate crew fired upon whalers near St. Lawrence Island.

The commander needed to take his ship to some port for surrender, but part of the crew wanted to put into a South American port, while others wanted to be landed in Australia or New Zealand.

After careful consideration, Lt. Waddell decided to run the gauntlet of federal cruisers and take his ship to a European port. He reached St. George's Channel on Nov. 5, without sighting any land on the way, 122 days after leaving the Aleutians.

On Nov. 6, *The Shenandoah* dropped anchor in Mersey off Liverpool, England. The crew hauled her flag down and surrendered her to the British government. The Brits eventually freed the officers and crew, and then turned the ship over to the United States.

ALASKA BECOMES A U.S. TERRITORY

9

SEWARD'S FOLLY BECOMES U.S. TREASURE

"Standing here and looking far off into the northwest, I see the Russian as he busily occupies himself in establishing seaports and towns and fortifications on the verge of the continent ... and I can say, 'Go on and build up your outposts all along the coast, up even to the Arctic Ocean; they will yet become the outposts of my own country – monuments of the civilization of the United States in the northwest!' "

So predicted U.S. Secretary of State William H. Seward in a memorable speech many years before the purchase of Alaska. That Alaska came into the possession of the United States was almost wholly due to Seward's foresight and persistent efforts.

The Imperial Government of Russia first approached the

U.S. Secretary of State William H. Seward saw the value of Alaska long before the United States purchased the territory in 1867.

U.S. government with a secret offer to sell its Russian possessions in America in 1859. The Russians had expended vast amounts of capital during the Crimean War in a futile struggle with France and England and needed to replenish the royal coffers.

However, with the Civil War raging during the early 1860s, the United States didn't pursue the purchase of Alaska until March 1867 when Seward received word that the Russians were ready to unload their northern property.

Treaty interrupts a game of whist

Seward was playing a game of whist with members of his family when he was interrupted by a late call from Russian Ambassador Baron Edouard de Stoeckl, who came to announce the arrival of a dispatch from St. Petersburg conveying the Emperor's assent to the cession of Alaska to the United States.

The Russians wanted "a cash payment of $7 million, with an additional $200,000 on condition that the cession should be free and unencumbered by any reservations, privileges, franchises or possessions by any associated companies, corporate or incorporate, Russian or any other."

CHARLES SUMNER.

U.S. Sen. Charles Sumner was among the minority who supported the purchase of Alaska.

The Secretary of State abandoned his game of whist. He and the Russian ambassador collected their clerks and had the treaty ready for transmission to the U.S. Senate by sunrise.

U.S. Sen. Charles Sumner, a Republican from Massachusetts, supported the transaction.

"The present treaty is a visible step in the occupation of the whole North American Continent; as such it will be recognized by the world, and accepted by the American people. But the treaty involves something more," Sumner said. "By it we dismiss one more monarch from this continent. One by one, they have retired; first France, then Spain, then France again, and now Russia – all giving way to that absorbing unity which is declared in the national motto, 'E pluribus Unum.' "

Some thought Alaska useless

But many other legislators didn't think the purchase was a good idea.

"... that Alaska was created for some purpose I have just as little doubt as I have had since the Rebellion of the necessity for the infernal regions ...," one member of Congress said. "The use and necessity for such a place as the infernal regions we now fully comprehend, but in relation to Alaska our information is so limited that conjecture can assign no use for it unless it was to demonstrate the folly to which those in authority are capable in the acquisition of useless territory."

With this letter, dated March 18, 1867, U.S. President Andrew Johnson authorized his Secretary of State, William H. Seward, to move forward and negotiate with Russian minister Edouard de Stoeckl for the purchase of Alaska.

Most Americans at the time thought the idea fantastic and ridiculous. Some asked, "How can there be anything of value in that barren, worthless, God-forsaken region?" Others said, "The only products are icebergs and polar bears," and "The ground is frozen six feet deep and the streams are glaciers."

What did the author of this "egregious blunder, palmed off on a silly administration by the shrewd Russians" see in the northern territory and why did Seward work so untiringly for its purchase?

Seward the expansionist

As Secretary of State during Abraham Lincoln's administration, Seward could see what disadvantage the United States labored under because we had no advance naval bases in the North Pacific. He saw that we would have a foothold there if Alaska was ours. In fact, Seward believed we should have not only Alaska, but many more bases in other parts of the world.

If Congress hadn't stopped him, we now might have the Virgin Islands, the Isthmus Canal Zone, Iceland and Greenland. Congress stopped him from acquiring Hawaii for free, but he did succeed in getting Alaska and the little, uninhabited, unknown island of Midway – Seward had the U.S. Navy take that island without saying anything to anyone.

Seward had long been an advocate of "Manifest Destiny" and was an expansionist at heart. The expansion of the United States to the ultimate edge of the North American shore and on to the islands of the Pacific had been his dream for years – even while serving as governor of New York, U.S. Senator, and finally, Secretary of State.

A forward thinker

Seward certainly wasn't in step with the majority of his country-men, however, who didn't think Alaska was such a good deal. Many said, "Why, we have land to burn and are short of ready cash."

Many years would pass before Seward's wisdom and foresight were appreciated as a piece of Far Eastern policy.

Seward also prophesied that European influence would wane and sink in importance while the Pacific would become the chief theater of importance in our future; this prediction was made in 1852 before there was a transcontinental railroad, telegraph line or even any Orient trade.

But Seward did more than predict. He began to make sure that the United States would occupy a place in the new scheme of things. He worked hard for a railroad to the Pacific and led the fight to get California into the Union.

Russia was expanding in the Pacific, too, trying to obtain bases in California and Hawaii. However, when it became apparent that sooner or later they would lose their American possessions, they were willing to cede them to the United States for a price rather than simply watch the hostile British gobble them up.

High-ranking officers in the Russian Navy were anxious not to have the Yankees, friendly or not, too close to the Russian mainland, so they recommended keeping the Kuriles and Commander Islands, although they were, economically, part of Alaska – thus preventing us from obtaining a toehold in Asia.

Sale of Alaska official

The treaty, which was adopted by the Senate in spite of fierce opposition and almost universal ridicule, was signed in May. The Russians handed Alaska over to the United States in Sitka in October 1867, following the arrival of several military and royal dignitaries.

Construction of Sitka's Baranof "castle," which was built with spruce logs, began in 1836 – 18 years after Baranof departed Sitka. It burned in 1894.

The U.S. troops that arrived at the Southeast seaport on the *John L. Stevens* from San Francisco on Oct. 9 were met by troops on the gunboats *Jamestown* and *Resaca*. After the *Ossipee* arrived in the afternoon of Oct. 18, Gen. Jefferson C. Davis, at the head of 250 men, marched up Baranof Hill where Alexander Andreevich Baranof's stronghold stood with the Imperial Eagles flag of Russia floating high above.

Maj. Gen. Jeff C. Davis took possession of Alaska from the Russians in October 1867. The general later hosted U.S. Secretary of State William H. Seward when Seward traveled to see the country he fought so hard to purchase.

Davis was met by U.S. Commissioner Gen. George Lovell Rousseau and Prince Dmitri Maksoutoff, acting chief manager and representative of Russia, his wife and others.

Ceremony marks transfer

The United States fired guns first, the Russians second, and so on in an alternating salute. The echoes reverberated from the sides of Mount Verstovy.

The Russian flag, as if reluctant to leave its proud position at the top of a lofty pine-tree staff, entangled itself in the halyards. Several men hoisted a U.S. Marine to the flag in a hastily rigged boatswain's chair, and detaching it, the soldier dropped the flag to the ground, where it was caught on the bayonets of Russian troops.

Another soldier raised the Stars and Stripes to take the place of the Russian flag, and again cannons boomed from ships in the harbor. This time the Russians led the salute.

Alexei Pestchouroff, the Commissioner of the Czar, spoke a few words of transfer. Then Gen. Rousseau signified his acceptance. With that ceremony, Alaska passed to the dominion of Uncle Sam and became part of the United States.

Russian princess weeps

The young and beautiful Princess Maksoutoff, wife of the last chief manager of the Russian-American Company, cried as the flag of her country was lowered.

"The Princess Maksoutoff wept at the spectacle, and all nature seemed to keep her company, drenching to the skin all the participants in the ceremony," an observer later said. "The native

Prince Maksoutoff, Russian governor of Alaska, handed Alaska over to the United States in October 1867 in Sitka.

Indians in their canoes witnessed it from a distance, listening stolidly to the booming of cannon, and gazing with indifference upon the descending and ascending flags. Of the nature of the proceedings, they had a faint and imperfect conception, but one thing they did realize – that the country they once imagined their own was now being transferred to a strange people, by what must have appeared to them a singular ceremony."

Once the transfer of Alaska to the United States from Russia was finalized, the Americans lost no time in converting the small seaport village of Sitka into a hot spot of capitalism.

The United States of America issued a check for $7.2 million for the purchase of Alaska in August 1867.

Capitalism flourishes in new U.S. territory

"A number of businessmen had accompanied or preceded the commissioners of the two Governments, and the American flag was scarcely floating from the top of the flagstaff before new shops were opened, vacant lots covered with the framework of shanties, and negotiations entered into for the purchase of houses, furs and other property of the old Russian-America Company, and in less than a week new stores had been erected, and two tenpin alleys, two drinking saloons and a restaurant were opened," one observer reported in "Our Northern Domain," by Dana Estes and Company, published in 1910.

"Sitka, the town that for two-thirds of a century had known nothing beyond the dull, unchanging routine of labor, and a scanty supply of necessaries at prices fixed by a corporate body eight or ten thousand miles away, was profoundly startled even by this small ripple of innovation."

Americans flock north

To the new American domain flocked a herd of men of all sorts and conditions – Alaskan pioneers and squatters, and aspirants for political honors and emoluments in the new territory. Before the first sunset gun was fired, preemption stakes dotted the ground, and the air was full of rumors of framing a "city charter," creating laws and remunerative offices, and it was not long before an election was held for town officers, at which more than 100 votes were polled for nearly as many candidates.

The Russian population looked with wonder on this new activity. The families of the higher officials, as well as those of the farmer

Once Sitka was transferred to the United States, Americans lost no time in starting new businesses, opening saloons and writing up new laws. This scene shows Lincoln Street looking west from the tower of St. Michael's Church with a tourist ship in port in 1897.

Some Russians felt the United States grabbed Alaska as part of an expansionist policy, and Baranof's Castle, sitting high on a hill with a view of the water, may have been a reminder of all they had lost.

and laboring classes, opened their houses to the newcomers with true Russian hospitality. But unfortunately they did not discriminate, treating officers, merchants and solders alike, and in many cases, their kindness was shamefully abused.

"Robberies and assaults were the order of the day, or rather of the night, until the peaceable inhabitants were compelled to lock their doors at nightfall, not daring to move about until the bugle sounded in the morning. ..."

The Russian-American Company was allowed two years to settle its affairs and transport those who wished to return to their home country. For this purpose, all its employees distributed throughout the territory congregated at Sitka. From the time of transfer to 1869, nearly 1,000 Russians were living there, receiving between $40,000 and $50,000 a month among them in salaries.

Those wages, regularly spent before the next pay day, made business brisk. In addition to the Russians, there also were two companies of soldiers and a few hundred American and other traders milling about the town, while a man-of-war and a revenue cutter sat anchored in the harbor. These sources of revenue yielded a golden harvest to businessmen and saloon keepers.

Russian thoughts on the transfer

How did the sellers feel later? In "Outline of Modern and Recent History of the U.S.A.," published by the Soviet Academy of Science in 1960, the authors wrote:

"… in the nineteenth century, the United States, exploiting the distance of Alaska from Russia, conducted an expansionist policy with regard to Russian possessions in America."

According to another account in a Soviet text book, published in Moscow in 1955, "Seward blackmailed the Russian Minister in Washington, Stoeckl, with threats of an invasion of American settlers in Alaska."

A mere $7.2 million, the Russians wistfully exclaim, was paid for this "huge territory – one that was shortly to be burgeoning with rich gold and coal deposits."

Seward ridiculed after purchase

The discovery of gold and other valuable resources were in the future, however, when Seward tried to educate his countrymen to the value of Alaska. He reminded them of the unfavorable comment that had been heaped upon Jefferson at the time of the purchase of the "desert waste of Louisiana" and "snake-infested Florida." But a torrent of abuse was unleashed on Seward and President Andrew Johnson – a campaign of ridicule and hostile criticism that endured for many years.

Seward became the target of bitter abuse, particularly after he helped Johnson adopt Lincoln's moderate Reconstruction policies. He stood by Johnson, too, during the latter's impeachment trial, thereby losing the respect of the leaders of his party. Toward the end of his second term as Secretary of State, he found himself almost alone.

"Grey, bent and weary," in the words of his son, he stood in the parlor of his Washington home one evening in 1868 and remarked on all the world rulers who had died or been deposed during his eight years in the State Department.

"I can only hope," he said with a wintry smile, "they all enjoyed the prospect of getting out of office as much as I do."

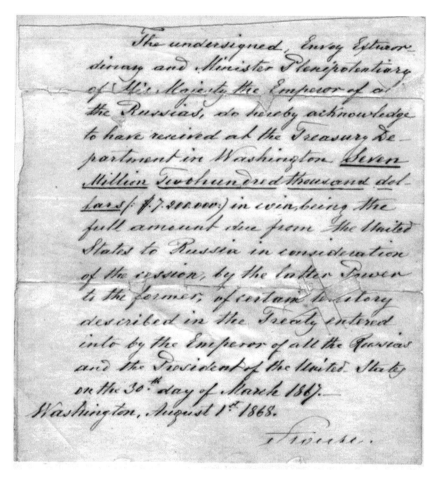

The receipt from "His Majesty, Emperor of all the Russias," dated Aug. 1, 1868, acknowledges the receipt of $7.2 million from the United States "for the purchase of territory described in the treaty" entered into by the President of the United States and the Emperor on March 30, 1867.

Seward travels to Alaska

Seward lived for three more years, spending them in world travel, including a trip to Sitka. He was entertained there by Gen. Davis, and then traveled to Lynn Canal where he was feasted with great hospitality at Klukwan. To Chief Klokutch of the village he gave a blanket woven in special emblems for the occasion. It remained one of the chief's most prized possessions until his death. To Seward's delight, the Natives he met called him "The Great Tyee" (Chief).

Seward still was looking into the future when in a speech at Sitka he said, "The political society to be constituted here, first as a territory, and ultimately as a state or many states, will prove a worthy constituency of the Republic."

When U.S. Secretary of State William H. Seward traveled to Klukwan in Southeast Alaska after the territory's purchase, he was treated with great hospitality. He gave Chief Klokutch a special blanket with American emblems, and perhaps feasted his eyes on beautiful ceremonial art as portrayed in this photograph of Gaanaxteidi clan artifacts displayed inside the Raven House in Klukwan.

He never faltered in his faith in the value of Alaska. It's even reported that when he'd retired to the quiet of his home in Auburn, N.Y., he was asked by a fellow townsman what he considered his greatest achievement as Secretary of State.

"The purchase of Alaska," Seward is alleged to have replied. "But it will take the country a generation to appreciate it."

Seward's foresight pays off

Indeed, many years would pass before Seward's gift to the nation was recognized. But after Dec. 7, 1941, when Japan attacked the United States at Pearl Harbor, Hawaii, his foresight and wisdom could not be argued.

Seward enabled America to become a Pacific as well as an Atlantic power. Before almost anyone else, he saw the importance of the Great Circle route; he early advocated a subsidy for a cable line to Siberia via the Bering Sea, and he is quoted as saying in 1846:

"Our population is destined to roll its resistless waves to the icy barriers of the north and to encounter oriental civilization on the shores of the Pacific."

And this was said even before the California gold rush sent the relentless tide of gold-seekers west, then north.

His prophecy that "Russian outposts in the Northwest would become outposts of the United States" came true.

One Confederate soldier could have altered Alaska's history

But one Confederate soldier could have changed the course of Alaska's history. When Seward accepted President Abraham Lincoln's offer to be his Secretary of State late in 1860, Seward made himself a target five years later when John Wilkes Booth decided to end the president's life.

And if Booth's co-conspirator had been successful, Alaska still might be under Russian rule today.

Booth, who assassinated Lincoln in 1865 at Ford's Theatre, had a larger plan in mind when he recruited a young Confederate "spy" who went by the name of Lewis Paine. Booth assigned Paine, whose birth name was Lewis Thornton Powell, and David Herold to kill Seward on April 14, at approximately 10:15 p.m., to coincide with Booth's attack on President Lincoln. At the same time, another conspirator named George Atzerodt was to assassinate Vice President Andrew Johnson at the Kirkwood House.

Why did Booth want Seward assassinated? Because if Andrew Johnson also had been killed as Booth planned, he thought the process of electing a new president would throw the Union into a state of "electoral chaos" if Seward were dead, too, since only the Secretary of State could set in motion the means for an election.

Letter from Abraham Lincoln to William H. Seward dated Dec. 8, 1860.

Paine and Herold showed up at Seward's home, called the Old Club House, in Lafayette Square and were admitted to the residence after they told the butler that they had medicine from Dr. Tullio Suzzaro Verdi for the Secretary of State. Seward, then 63, lay in bed in his third-floor bedroom suffering from cuts, bruises, a dislocated shoulder and broken jaw, which had resulted from a recent carriage accident.

Armed with a large, heavy 1858 Whitney revolver hidden in his pocket, the 6-foot, 1-1/2-inch Paine climbed the steps toward his target. He encountered Seward's son, Frederick, who was Assistant Secretary of State at the time, and attempted to shoot him. But his revolver misfired, so he pistol-whipped the young man who blocked his path. Frederick slumped to the floor.

Paine then pulled out his huge silver Bowie knife, which had an alligator motif and the engraving "The Hunter's Companion – Real Life Defender." He raced to the third floor, crashed through Seward's bedroom door and jumped on the injured Secretary. He slashed repeatedly at the elderly statesman's neck and face. One stab wound went all the way through the Secretary's right cheek. Although seriously injured in the attack, Seward's life may have been saved by the leather-covered iron brace around his neck and jaw.

Seward's nurse, Sgt. George F. Robinson, an invalid U.S. Marine, tried to pull Paine off Seward with the assistance of Seward's other son, Augustus.

Paine broke free and bolted down the stairs. As he raced outside, he realized that Herold had deserted him, but had left Paine's horse tied to a tree. The would-be-assassin calmly untied the animal, mounted and rode away. Paine then hid out in a wooded lot about a mile from the Navy Yard Bridge.

Three days later, he was captured by detectives after he showed up at a boarding house used by Confederate secret agents. Paine was slapped into irons and charged with conspiracy and attempted murder.

This woodcut engraving from the National Police Gazette depicts Paine's attack on Secretary of State William H. Seward on April 14, 1865.

Paine's lawyer, William E. Doster, argued in vain that Paine "at the time had no will of his own, but had surrendered his will completely to Booth." He was found guilty and sentenced to hang.

Paine went to the gallows on July 7, 1865.

And Seward went on to negotiate the purchase of Alaska from Russia.

In the Great Land he worked so hard to obtain for the United States, our appreciation is shown by his name given to a city, a peninsula, a glacier, a mountain range and a passage. In March, Seward's Day is a state holiday, in memory of the day on which Seward signed the treaty of Alaska's purchase.

This rare photograph shows William H. Seward's disfigured face after Paine's attack.

10

Apostle to the North

Around the time that Alaska was changing from Russian to American hands, one English Espiscopalian was beginning a long and arduous path toward becoming a much-loved religious teacher in the Yukon and Alaska.

In one of the loveliest and most secluded spots in the Yukon is a humble grave overlooking the lake at Carcross. An Indian woodsman cut down and trimmed rough fir for the fence that encloses it, then fixed it firm and stable. The gray granite headstone bears the inscription, "In the peace of Christ."

The man who lies beneath that headstone is William Carpenter Bompas, the First Bishop of Athabasca, First Bishop of MacKenzie River and First Bishop of the Yukon. Church officials said that "in the history of the Church of England, there is no parallel to such a career."

His career started in England. He was the fourth son of that English lawyer on whom Charles Dickens modeled his Sergeant Buzfuz in "Pickwick Papers." One evening in 1865, Bompas attended a missionary meeting where the speaker told of the vast lands of Canada and the need for missionaries, particularly one lonely station on the Yukon where Rev. Robert McDonald, a pioneer missionary, was hanging on despite failing health.

"Shall no one come forward to take up the standard of the Lord as it falls from his hands?" the speaker asked.

Bompas travels North

One man was ready. His heart had been deeply touched, and he walked at once to the vestry. Bompas, then a Lincolnshire curate, offered to go relieve the missionary on the Yukon.

He had only three weeks to prepare for the long journey, but it was ample. His brother later told of his giving away all his books and tokens of remembrance in order not to take anything that would lead his thoughts back home. When told it was about 8,000 miles away and would take about a year to reach, a smile passed over Bompas' face as he replied, "I see I must start with a small bag."

Bompas traveled from Liverpool to New York, then headed westward by way of Chicago and the Red River to Fort Chipewyan. That's where the real hazards of the voyage began.

William Carpenter Bompas, the First Bishop of Athabasca, First Bishop of MacKenzie River and First Bishop of the Yukon, came north from England in 1865.

With winter approaching, he and three Indians started a dangerous canoe trip. The river soon became full of floating ice, which became a solid mass of ice from bank to bank. The men finally cached the canoe and pushed on by foot with winter upon them and very little food. When they saw the lights of Fort Resolution at Great Slave Lake, it was a welcome sight.

Bompas reaches Fort Simpson

On Christmas morning, 178 days after leaving London, Bompas and his dog team pulled into Fort Simpson, Yukon Territory, where he stayed until Easter. He spent his time at the fort learning the language of the Native people so he could preach to them in their own tongue.

His next voyage was to Fort Norman and up the Peace River to Fort Vermillion, the scene of his first labors. His relief of McDonald on the Yukon would have to wait, he felt, as he plunged into visiting Native camps, journeying hundreds of miles and constantly studying the Native languages. In 1870, he decided to visit Eskimos farther north, and with two Eskimo guides, started his journey to the Arctic.

Plagued by snow blindness, it was one of his most difficult trips. For three days of awful darkness, he was led by the hand of one of the Eskimos, but after a day of rest in an Eskimo camp, he

Bishop William Carpenter Bompas lived among the Eskimos during his first years in the North Country and kept them in mind for the rest of his life.

regained his sight. His great friend among the Eskimos was old Chief Shipatoutook, whose son, many years later, remembered and talked of the white man who had lived with his father.

Never again was Bompas able to visit the band of Eskimos along the MacKenzie River, but he always held them in mind and declared, "There's nothing warmer than the grasp of a husky's hand."

Journeys lead to Rev. McDonald

Endless journeys occupied the next three years, including a 16-week canoe trip to Fort Vermillion, where he vaccinated more than 500 Natives against a smallpox epidemic. He worked his way to the headwaters of the Peace, back by way of Hay River to Fort McPherson, and over the mountains to the Yukon, at last, where he was called to become Bishop of the Yukon.

It took Bompas more than five years to travel by ship, canoe, on foot and by dog sled from London to the Yukon to relieve a now-healthy Rev. Robert McDonald in 1870.

In 1873, he made a trip back to London for his consecration and returned to the Yukon with a bride, Charlotte Selina, who was as remarkable as the bishop himself.

The daughter of an English doctor, Charlotte was raised in Italy, where she had enjoyed elegant parties and had even danced with the king at her first ball. Full of spirit, she was artistic and musical. Her life as Bishop Bompas' helpmate took her into the most remote lands on earth – her former life must have seemed like a dream.

On May 12, 1874, they set off for Canada – never again was Bishop Bompas to see his native land. The northern wilds needed him and there he stayed until the end.

Bompas manages diocese

The couple first settled at Fort Simpson, situated on the confluence of the MacKenzie and Liard rivers, the most central point for managing the vast diocese of a million square miles. Years before their arrival, the Hudson Bay Company had occupied it and in 1859 a church and mission house were built.

Fort Yukon, located just north of the Arctic Circle, was home for Bishop William Carpenter Bompas for many years before the Klondike Gold Rush.

Bompas especially loved the children of his flock and enjoyed teaching them, although they often taxed his patience. One of the lessons they learned was how far they could push him. When they saw the good bishop running his fingers through his hair (what he had left), they knew a storm was brewing and silence would ensue.

Like Robert McDonald, Bompas had a talent for languages and quickly learned to communicate in many of the Native dialects. Between 1870 and 1880, he composed four primers in Slavi, Beaver, Dogrib and Gwich'in languages. He wanted his clergy to converse well with the Native people, too, so he insisted that new clergy spend at least four hours a day in language study.

Stationed at Fort Yukon many years before the gold rush, Bompas had seen so much gold on a small river near the fort that he could have gathered it with a spoon. But he only was intent on translating prayer books for the Indians, not the metal that was to cause such change in the North Country.

Bishop William Carpenter Bompas spent most of his life ministering to the people in the Yukon Territory.

Over the next several years he managed his diocese, and as miners moved in and the population grew, he sectioned off the regions for other missionaries. By the early 1890s he was in charge of the region west of the Rocky Mountains and called it the Diocese of Selkirk – which is now the Yukon.

Bompas settles at Fortymile

During spring 1892, after the ice went out, Bompas traveled down the Porcupine River to the Yukon to meet his wife, who had been in England. They reunited at a Native village on the river, and she later wrote that when she saw her husband, whom she hadn't seen for several years, he was "grey, weather beaten, but in health better than I had expected."

By 1895, Bompas and his wife had settled into Fortymile, where there was a large camp of miners and Natives. He described his new See City as having "two doctors, library, reading room, debating society, theatre, eating houses and plenty of saloons, two stores and a few tradesmen. One debate was as to what had caused the most misery in the last century – war or whisky. It was decided to give the unenviable preference to whisky – truly appropriate to the mining camp."

The miners had a profound respect for the bishop and his wife. As a token of their esteem, they presented Charlotte with a splendid gold nugget on one Christmas day for being "the first white lady who has wintered among us."

While ministering to this group of miners, the bishop was unaware that an event was taking place in his diocese that, in a few years, would change his whole missionary work in the Yukon.

Gold discovery changes mission

About 50 miles upstream from Fortymile is the Klondike River, and George Washington Carmack, along with several Native companions, discovered gold along its banks in 1896. That famous discovery electrified the world and brought thousands into the Yukon to seek the precious metal.

"For myself during the past winter I have devoted my days to digging the mines of God's holy Word, and have found, in my own estimation, prizes richer than the nuggets of the Klondike," Bompas wrote.

However his hands were busy with the men who had been drawn to search for those Klondike nuggets.

The bishop's burden of responsibility greatly increased with the advent of the white man. The population of his diocese increased sevenfold at rapid strides. And besides providing for the spiritual needs of these people, Bompas felt compelled to keep the Natives away from the vices of the white man like whisky and gambling.

Caribou Crossing, later named Carcross, is where Bishop William Carpenter Bompas spent the remainder of his life teaching and living a frugal existence.

When a church was built in the new gold city of Dawson, Bompas attended to both. However, once he made a trip back to Fortymile where he was laid low by a severe attack of scurvy. Meanwhile, his wife had been stranded at Fort Yukon for eight months and to Bompas came word of riotous times among the miners there and their desperate efforts to overpower the soldiers in order to obtain food. He was most thankful when the ice went out of the Yukon and Charlotte was able to rejoin him. Fresh vegetables cleared up his scurvy.

Bompas moves to Carcross

In the summer of 1897, the bishop turned his attention to the southwest part of his diocese at Caribou Crossing, later named Carcross, at the head of Lake Bennett. He and his wife first lived in a tent, and later bought a bunkhouse, which was infested with rats and mice, for $50. A visitor in 1903 wrote:

"... built of logs on sand ... flooring boards half an inch apart, roof papered with battens across the paper. Ventilation carried to excess. Everything around as simple as indifference to creature comforts can make it, excepting for the books, which are numerous, up to date, and as choice as any excellent scholars could wish for."

The bishop had started a small school and home for orphans and neglected children at Fortymile. He moved it to Caribou Crossing, and the school filled his time.

Visitors said it was an interesting sight to see the venerable white-haired teacher among the Native children. He's been described as "a giant of a man, with a high dome, a hawk nose, piercing eyes and the flowing beard of Moses."

Creature comforts always had meant nothing to the ascetic bishop. He ignored all dainties, drank his sugarless coffee from a tin cup and his knife was the only utensil he ever used. He never took any holidays, and it was said he thought nothing of making a present of his trousers to a man without pants and then mushing home in his red flannels.

Bishop's labors end in Carcross

His work at Carcross proved to be in the evening of his labors. Symptoms of some loss of strength and vigor in this strong man began to show. He needed stronger and stronger glasses. Since his last attack of scurvy, he had lost all sense of taste and smell. He often was heard to mutter to himself, "Courage, courage." More than one of his friends received the impression that he had not long to live.

Sitting on a box on the evening of June 9, 1906, the 72-year-old bishop began writing the sermon that would be his last. Then the pen stopped. He stood and leaned his elbows on a pile of boxes. Suddenly the body, which had stood so much, fell forward. His labors were over.

After Bishop Bompas was buried beside the lake at Carcross, his wife returned to England, but came back after a year. She lived in Montreal, but traveled to the mission school at Carcross every year and brought presents she collected, made or bought. In 1917, a month before her 87th birthday, she quietly fell into eternal asleep.

SEA OTTER HUNTERS

Guy F. Cameron

Ivan Petroff, Alaska's first census-taker, traveled by boats, sleds and umiaks to many parts of Alaska to assess the number and types of people populating the United States' new territory in 1880.

11

Alaska's mysterious first census-taker

An unofficial head count taken at Sitka by the U.S. Army in 1869 revealed 391 civilians made up the town's population, which included 10 saloon keepers and 29 prostitutes. It was hoped that the 1880 Census would elevate Alaska's image.

Chosen to take the important tally was one of the most controversial figures in Alaska history, Ivan Petroff. Years later, historians would say Petroff was everything from a "Prevaricator Par Excellence" and able historian, to a three-time Army deserter, falsifier of documents and "teller of tall tales."

Petroff faced many obstacles to his newly appointed mission. No one knew how large the territory of Alaska was, and there were no roads, only a few Native trails. Travel by water also was at a minimum. A mail steamer reached Sitka only once a month, and other than a few revenue cutters and Native bidarkas, canoes and umiaks, there were few sailing vessels.

Government was hardly existent in Alaska during this time. By 1878 all the Army posts had been abandoned, and by 1880 there were only two post offices in Alaska – one in Sitka and one in Wrangell. While there were a few U.S. Customs collectors and inspectors, there wasn't a single municipal government and no newspapers.

With no roads, and only a few Native trails, Alaska's first census-taker, Ivan Petroff, traveled around some parts of the territory in skin boats called bidarkas. These Native men, complete with harpoons, are paddling toward a ship in Cold Bay.

Petroff tackles monumental task

When we think of the task faced by Petroff more than 100 years ago, we can only marvel that he accomplished as much as he did. He got to only around half of the vast territory and had to depend upon whaling captains, traders, U.S. Signal Service personnel, Russian Church records, priests, missionaries and merchants for help in acquiring statistics.

He traveled about 8,700 miles by kayaks and open boats. Petroff's count totaled 33,426 people, including 430 Caucasians, 1,756 Creoles, 17,617 Inuit, 2,145 Aleut, 3,927 Tinneh, 6,763 Tlingits and 788 Haidas.

Of course, his figures were questioned – especially in Southeast – and there were official protests of a short count. But as Ted C. Hinckley wrote:

"If Petroff had had a dozen or so competent field workers and the finest of land and water transportation, he might have been able to do it in five years."

Gov. Swineford said Petroff was perhaps the most knowledgeable man for the job.

Who was Ivan Petroff?

Petroff was described by his contemporaries as "tall, spare, blond, reserved and reticent — but bright, well informed and very skilled in translating."

Born in St. Petersburg, Russia, in 1812, he lost his father, a Russian army officer, in the Crimean War. Petroff came to the United States in 1861, enlisted in the Army and soon deserted.

Ivan Petroff traveled close to 9,000 miles by kayaks and open boats counting 33,426 people in 1880. He made his way up creeks and rivers and counted all those he encountered, like this Athabascan woman and her sleeping baby at a temporary summer camp.

He re-enlisted at Fort Colville, Washington Territory, as a private in Battery F, 2nd U.S. Artillery, but when his company was posted to Alaska in June 1868, he deserted once more. Authorities arrested and imprisoned him.

However, Petroff was released when his battery commander needed an interpreter to deal with the Russian-speaking population at his post. By 1869, he was in Fort Kenai, the old Redoubt St. Nicholas, and stayed there until his discharge in 1870.

Another enlistment led to one more desertion and imprisonment, but he was freed after a California senator interceded. Soon after, Petroff went to work for Hubert Howe Bancroft and probably wrote much, perhaps more than a quarter, of Bancroft's "History of Alaska, 1730-1885."

Petroff becomes Alaska authority

While gathering and writing material for Bancroft, Petroff began acquiring his reputation as an Alaska authority but lost his reputation as a journalist. He passed off newspaper articles as his own about the Turko-Russian War. His journalistic career ended when people discovered that he had copied the stories from European papers.

He continued working for Bancroft, however, and in 1878 sailed on the U.S. Revenue Cutter *Richard Bush* for Alaska to obtain material for Bancroft's history.

Petroff added to his reputation as an Alaska authority by testifying before a Senate Committee on Territories concerning civil government in Alaska. Soon after his appearance before the committee, he was appointed to take the 1880 Alaska Census.

His census-taking odyssey began in June 1880, when he sailed north from San Francisco for the Aleutians, Shumagins and Pribiloff islands and St. Michael. On July 13, he began his ascent of the Yukon in a kayak pulled by a steamer.

He traveled in a bidarka on his return trip with two Natives rowing hard against the current. He stopped at Nukluk, now Tanana, and then downstream to present-day Russian Mission. He portaged to the Kuskokwim and from its mouth traveled southward along Bristol

Bay to Naknek. Next he traversed the Alaska Peninsula to Katmai and crossed to Kodiak, where he took a ship to San Francisco for the winter.

Petroff heads to Southeast

In 1881, Petroff went to the Southeastern Gulf of Alaska shores and the Panhandle and spent several weeks in Wrangell. Officials had been told to cooperate with him, and although Alaska was officially "dry," he was allowed to bring whiskey for his personal use — perhaps to better withstand the rigors of his task. According to missionary S. Hall Young, Petroff was known in Wrangell as "Hollow Legs" because of his capacity.

The census-taker claimed to have put in two seasons on the Yukon, but historian Morgan Sherwood questions whether he could

In 1881, Ivan Petroff went to Southeastern Alaska shores and spent several weeks counting people in that region. Potlatches like this one in Klukwan could have offered him a plentiful count of Tlingit Indians.

have had time for a second investigation and also questions his account of being held captive by Chugach Indians in 1881, which, he said, prevented him from "making a more complete execution of his duties."

All in all, though, it was an epic undertaking and the knowledge he acquired is embodied in his "Report on the Population, Industries and Resources of Alaska," published as part of the 10th Census. Sherwood called it one of the three most influential books on Alaska published in the 19th century — the others being Bancroft's "History of Alaska" and William Healy Dall's "Alaska and its Resources" — and was used in documents in 1950 to determine legal status of Alaska's Natives.

Petroff appointed deputy collector

In 1883, Petroff was appointed deputy collector of customs at Kodiak and held that post until 1887. About this time, the U.S. Secretary of War was persuaded to clear him of desertion charges, so that troublesome chapter in his past was closed. In 1890, he was hired as a special agent to direct the 1890 Census. This time there were eight men to help him count the population.

Petroff's prestige was high. He was introduced to President Harrison by pioneer missionary Sheldon Jackson, but he was shortly to undergo another disgrace. In 1892 he was in Washington, D.C., to write up the 1890 Census and was borrowed by the State Department to help translate documents from the Russian-American Company in connection with the fur seal controversy between the United States and Great Britain.

It was discovered that he had altered and added to the original documents. He confessed when confronted with the evidence, and again was disgraced. He dropped out of sight, living in Pennsylvania and earning a livelihood by translating, using his mother's name of Lanen, and also tried his hand at writing short stories. He died in 1896 at Philadelphia.

With all his faults, he was clearly a talented man, said Alaska historian Robert Pierce. It was a Herculean task confronting him in that

1880 Census, but his report was a positive contribution. He helped inform others of the value and needs of Alaska, and Pierce said he gave the government its first comprehensive look at the population of its new territory.

And a major discovery that same year gave the world a look at what the new territory held along some of its creeks.

Alaska's first census-taker settled in Kodiak in 1883 after being appointed deputy collector of customs. Ivan Petroff later directed the 1890 Census.

12

GOLD FOUND IN SOUTHEAST

While Ivan Petroff was busy collecting the 1880 Census in an attempt to assess Alaska's population, others were about to make a discovery that would turn men's thoughts to gold.

Chief Kowee led Joseph Juneau and Richard T. Harris to gold around Juneau in 1880.

Small amounts of gold had been found in 1848 along the Russian River on the Kenai Peninsula and during the 1870s in the Cassiar district in Canada. Some prospectors found a bit of gold ore around Sitka and Windham Bay, too. But it wasn't until 1880 that a major find in Southeast Alaska would start bringing prospectors by the droves into the North Country.

Auk Indian Chief Kowee, who lived on Admiralty Island, found a yellowish ore in the ground that July. He took a sample to Sitka, where an engineer named George Pilz had offered to reward those who could lead his mining teams to gold. The

When Auk Indian Chief Kowee discovered gold nuggets in the Silver Bow Basin area of Southeast Alaska, he traveled to Sitka, shown here in 1886, where he hoped to claim his due from George Pilz, an engineer who had offered to reward those who could lead his mining teams to gold.

chief sought the reward so he could purchase blankets, food and other goods for his people.

Based on the chief's sample, Pilz grubstaked two veteran prospectors, Joe Juneau and Richard Harris, and sent them on their way with the chief to locate the source of the ore.

However, not too far into their trip, the prospectors traded their rations with the Indians for home brew – called hootchinoo. Consequently, they never got far from the beach and eventually returned to Sitka empty-handed.

Chief Kowee returned to Sitka, too. And he brought more ore with him, as well as an account of how the miners had spent their grubstake.

Pilz sent the two men back with the chief, who some said literally dragged the reluctant prospectors up Gold Creek to what later became Silver Bow Basin.

In October 1880, the men struggled through dripping moss, slippery rocks and devil's club to get to a place the Tlingits called Bear's Nest.

"We followed the gulch down from the summit of the mountain into the basin," Richard Harris later wrote. "It was a beautiful sight to see the large pieces of quartz, of black sulfide and galena all spangled over with gold."

Prospectors establish town site

The next day, Harris wrote out a code of laws for the new mining district, and on Oct. 18, he and Juneau established a 160-acre town site on the beach and called it Harrisburgh.

OLD TILLICUM
R. T. Harris   Joe Juneau

They loaded about 1,000 pounds of gold ore into their canoe and returned to Sitka, although there are conflicting reports about the route they took. Some accounts say the men paddled directly to Sitka. Others say the men actually headed south toward Canada and representatives of Pilz met them en route and brought them back to Sitka at gunpoint.

The portraits of Richard Tighe Harris and Joe Juneau appeared on an Old Tillicum cigar box circa 1900.

Wherever the truth lay, the discovery of gold in that rich basin began Alaska's first big gold rush, 16 years before the Klondike.

And what began as a mining camp, with about 40 prospectors in an area with 640 Auk Indians and 269 Taku at Douglas, quickly turned into the first town to be founded in Alaska after the purchase of the territory from the Russians in 1867.

The influx of white prospectors changed the dynamics of the area by leaps and bounds. Trading posts, breweries and saloons popped up overnight, and by March 1881, monthly steamship service was bringing in supplies to the placer miners along Gastineau Channel.

"Glory Hole" yields tons of gold

Most placer miners were taking out between $16 and $80 a day in gold from the town that changed its name from Harrisburgh to Pilzburg to Rockwell. The final name, Juneau, stuck after Joe Juneau used his first summer's earnings to buy round after round of drinks

The Treadwell Glory Hole became one of the largest quartz lode mines in the world. It was so deep that men working at the bottom and along the sides appeared no larger than flies when one looked down on them from the top.

to get his fellow miners to vote to change the name.

Sounds from the first ore-crushing mill were heard in 1882, after a gambler's hunch compelled John Treadwell to purchase a claim from Pierre Joseph "French Pete" Erussard.

Erussard, a Canadian prospector who thought his find of an outcrop of gold-bearing quartz marginal, only asked Treadwell for $400. He just needed enough money to pay for goods to stock his new general store.

Treadwell, a carpenter and builder by trade, had several years of experience in both placer and lode mines in California and Nevada before he came to Alaska. He'd been in charge of construction of a home for a San Francisco banker when news of the gold strike on Gastineau Channel arrived. The banker and other investors paid Treadwell's expenses to look over the prospects in the fall of 1881.

Treadwell's decision to buy Erussard's claim on Douglas Island turned into the discovery of the famed "Glory Hole."

Treadwell Mine, which started with five stamp machines to crush ore, grew over time to use 960 stamps and became one of the largest quartz lode mines in the world. It was so deep that men working at the bottom and along the sides barely could be seen.

Firsthand account of Glory Hole

Ella Higginson visited the Glory Hole and recounted her experience of dropping down into the mine in 1905.

" … there was barely room on the rather dirty 'lift' for us. We stood very close together. It was dark as a dungeon," she wrote in her book, "Alaska: The Great Country."

"As we started, I clutched somebody – it did not matter whom. I also drew one wild and amazed breath; before I could possibly let go of that one – to say nothing of drawing another – there was a bump, and we were in a level 1,080 feet below the surface of the earth.

"We stepped out into a brilliantly lighted station, with a high, glittering quartz ceiling," Higginson continued. "The swift descent had so affected my hearing that I could not understand a word that was spoken for fully five minutes."

The scenes that met Higginson's eyes included shafts, ore bins, drifts, levels, stations where quartz-laden cars passed and stopes, which were areas where the ore was removed.

Tram cars, each drawn by a single horse, carried ore from one location to another.

Horses and men work the mine

"One horse had been in the mine seven years without once seeing sunlight or fields of green grass," Higginson wrote. "But every man passing one of these horses gave him an affectionate pat, which was returned by a low, pathetic whinny of recognition and pleasure.

"Each man worked by the light of a single candle (in a dark stope). They were stoping out ore and making it ready to be dumped into lower levels – from which it could finally be hoisted out of the mine in skips.

Hydraulic mining became big business in Silver Bow Basin near Juneau.

"The ceiling was so low that we could walk only in a stooping position. The laborers worked in the same position; and what with this discomfort and the insufficient light, it would seem that their condition was unenviable. Yet their countenances denoted neither dissatisfaction nor ill-humor."

In 1889, the Alaska Treadwell Gold Mining Company bought out John Treadwell and his investors for $4 million. Treadwell returned to California, where he became associated with his brother, James, and started a trust company that went broke. In 1914, Treadwell filed for bankruptcy in New York City and died in a hotel there in 1927 at the age of 85.

The Alaska-Treadwell Gold Mining Company took out gold valued at $21,817,296.19 between 1885 and 1904. Two men at the left stand near a cube that represents Alaska's purchase price of $7.2 million.

Miners flock to Juneau-Douglas

The Treadwell organization, which included four mines called the Treadwell, 700-foot, Mexican and Ready Bullion, operated for 36 years and produced $66 million worth of gold. A cave-in and extensive flooding in 1917 brought its era of prosperity to an end.

But the early success of the Treadwell mine brought a couple thousand miners to Southeast Alaska. N.A. Fuller staked a claim on Granite Creek that became the site of the first hard rock mine in the 125-mile-long Juneau Gold Belt, and by the time of the Klondike Gold Rush, he'd incorporated into the Alaska Juneau Gold Mining Company.

Rich placer claims also were staked. During the 1880s, the Gold Mountain Company brought in a dozen burros from Mexico and started packing ore down the trail from Silver Bow Basin. Once it reached the channel, it was stowed on a steamship and carried to a San Francisco smelter. The mine later became known as Perseverance.

A few years after Higginson visited the Glory Hole in Southeast Alaska, a miner named George Washington Carmack traveled through town. But he thought Juneau had no prospects for a prospector, so he moved on to the Yukon and later made a discovery that started a near endless stream of hopeful miners to the North County.

But before that happened, Lt. Frederick Schwatka floated the mighty Yukon River and mapped its winding waters.

13

EXPLORING THE NILE OF ALASKA

In the summer of 1883, Lt. Frederick Schwatka traversed the upper Yukon River by raft from the lakes at its source to Fort Selkirk, about 500 miles, to gather information about the Indian tribes in the region, as well as study geographical details.

CANOEING UP THE DAYAY

This drawing from "A Summer in Alaska," by Frederick Schwatka, shows about a dozen canoes and Natives paddling through the Lynn Canal as Schwatka's group of explorers made their way to a fast-running stream called Dayay by the Indians.

The middle Yukon, as far as the junction with the Porcupine River, and the lower Yukon had already been explored by folks associated with the Russian-American Company who had ascended the stream to St. Michael.

Schwatka and his team, which included Dr. Wilson, topographical assistant Homan, Sgt. Gloster, Cpl. Shircliff, Pvt. Roth and Mr. McIntosh, as well as a myriad of Indian guides, left Chilkat June 7 with 13 canoes towed by a steam launch belonging to the Northwest Trading Company. The group passed through the Lynn Canal and the Chilkoot Inlet and arrived at the mouth of a swift-running stream, called the Dayay by the Indians.

LIEUTENANT SCHWATKA.

The U.S. Army commissioned Lt. Frederick Schwatka to find out what he could about the great river of the North, the mighty Yukon.

The party reached the headwaters of navigation on June 10, where they unloaded the canoes and packed tons of freight on the backs of 70 Indians. The party then reached the headwaters of the stream that evening, under banks of snow, at the foot of a pass about 3,000 feet high, which Schwatka named Perrier Pass.

"… long finger-like glaciers of clear blue ice extended down the granite gulches to our very level," he wrote in an 1885 article published in Century Magazine.

Schwatka builds a raft

His group next ascended the mountainside and arrived at the summit without mishap. They descended the pass and came in sight of two large lakes connected by a channel about a mile long. Schwatka named the bodies of water Lindermann and Bennett.

The men built a raft, 15 feet by 40 feet, on the shore of Lake Bennett and launched their expedition of the upper Yukon on the morning of June 19 onboard the *Resolute*.

As well as learning about the flora and fauna abundant on the route, Schwatka also learned something about the trading habits of the Indians who occupied that portion of the country.

"... At one time, when we had rowed ashore to avoid a sudden head-breeze, our Indians carelessly set fire to some of the dry, dead spruce timber, and the flames, enveloping the living trees for hours afterwards, sent upward dense volumes of smoke that we saw from many miles beyond," he wrote in his article. "Toward evening, some 15 or 20 miles ahead, a smoke was seen curling upward, and our Indians told us that it was an answer to the one we had accidentally made on Lake Bove."

Along his journey toward Fort Selkirk, Lt. Frederick Schwatka learned that the Chilkats crossed the Kotusk Mountains and traded with the Tagish Indians twice a year. Perhaps some of the regalia or other possessions of the dancers at this Klukwan potlatch came from those trading forays.

Schwatka tells of traders past

"These signal-smokes were quite common between the Chilkats and Tahk-heesh (Tagish) Indians, the former thus announcing to the latter that they had crossed the mountains and were in their country for trading purposes. An old trader on the Middle and Lower Yukon told me that this Chilkat-Tahk-heesh traffic was so great some years ago, that as many as 80 of the former tribe have been known to cross the Kotusk mountains by the Chilkat and Chilkoot trails twice a year; or, in brief, eight tons of trading material found its way over Perrier Pass and, ramifying from this as a center, spread over the whole northwest.

"Fort Selkirk, for a brief period a Hudson's Bay Company post, interfered with this commerce; but a war party of Chilkats in 1851 extended their trading tour 500 miles in order to burn it to the ground, and the blackened chimneys still standing in a thick grove of poplars are monuments that attest how well they did their work. ..."

Schwatka also complained in the article that the British maps of 1883 showed the Yukon River flowing into the Arctic Ocean, not too far west of the MacKenzie River, and that even the Russians were not sure that the immense delta, 30 or 40 miles south of St. Michael, was the same river on which they had established missions and fur trading factories at Nulato and Russian Mission.

Three-month journey ends

It took Schwatka about three months to float the almost 2,000 miles to the delta, although his raft-journey of more than 1,300 miles came to an end at the trading station of Nuklakayet.

"As we dragged the raft upon the bank, and left it there to burn out its existence as firewood, we felt that we were parting from a true and trusty friend," he wrote.

His party boarded a small-decked schooner called a "barka," and left the trading village on Aug. 8. The barka drifted until a little trading steamer came down the river and took the barka in tow. It brought the group to "a mission where an old Greek church of the Russian Company still drew subsidies from Russia." The following day they reached an Eskimo village, where they slept under a roof for the first time since spring.

The group arrived in Koatlik, at the mouth of the river, on Aug. 28, and two days later landed at St. Michael.

Schwatka's exploration of the Yukon River gave the world a first-hand account of the river and the lay of the land.

But while he was busy documenting the tribes and wealth of nature in the region, others were busy searching for wealth that sparkled along the river's banks.

Lt. Frederick Schwatka ended his three-month, nearly 2,000-mile float down the Yukon River at St. Michael, shown here, where he boarded a steamship and left Alaska. Notice the many riverboats in the background, behind this old Russian block house.

14

OLD JOHN BREMNER

While Lt. Frederick Schwatka's expedition was traversing the Yukon River toward Fort Selkirk, an old Scotsman was busy exploring the Copper River Valley, where a river later was named for him.

In the Koyukuk country, another river and lake are named after the grizzled old prospector, too. Bremner River, John River and Old John Lake all bear witness to the fact that John Bremner was there.

Not much is known of Bremner's life before he arrived in the North Country, but his death triggered a very exciting chapter in the history of Alaska. The hijacking of a Yukon River steamer, a wild chase on the Koyukuk, a miners' trial and frontier justice for Bremner's murderer make a story that could have been written by Rex Beach or Jack London.

Bremner's journal, sent to the trader at Nuchek in Prince William Sound, gives a graphic account of his stay at Taral – he was the first white man to winter with the Copper Indians – or "Ma Nuskas" as he called them. One entry, dated Oct. 14, 1884, gives a little information about his life before coming to Alaska. In his own original spelling, he wrote:

"I have been with the Negros in Africa and the natives of Australa (sic) and among the Indians of the plains, but of all the ... devils I ever was with, the Ma Nuska can beat them two to one. ..."

Bremner finds slim pickings at Taral

His stay at Taral – near Chitina – during the 1880s is a saga of hardships and privation. By spring he was tightening his belt one notch every other day. He was "a picture of wretchedness and destitution," wrote Lt. Henry Allen, the next white man up the Copper River. Allen was on an exploring trip that took him to the Tanana, Koyukuk and Yukon rivers – one of the most important reconnaissance voyages ever undertaken in Alaska. Bremner was easily persuaded to go along, since his prospecting along the Copper had been unsuccessful, and he thought it was a chance to seek greener pastures.

And he thought he'd reached those pastures when the party came to Koyukuk country. That's when he and Peder Johnson, another member of Allen's group, decided to leave the lieutenant's exploration party and go prospecting instead.

One particular tributary of the Koyukuk, which is a tributary of the Yukon River, John liked and talked about so much, that Johnson started calling it "Old John's river." It is marked on present-day maps as "John River."

Both Bremner and Johnson were convinced the gold that had escaped them so far was here, and they spent the summer of 1886 searching for nuggets. In the spring of 1887, they left Nuklukyet on the

Old John Bremner briefly joined the expedition of Lt. Henry Allen, shown here in the middle, during the early 1880s. The others pictured are Pvt. Fickett, left, and Sgt. Robertson.

John Bremner lived a life of hardship among the Copper River Indians during the 1880s.

Tanana River, where they'd spent the winter, and prospected along the river and its tributaries. They found colors, made rockers and took out enough gold for a grubstake for another year. When they reached the upper river in 1888, John decided to do some more extensive prospecting.

Old John meets an untimely fate

"Help me whipsaw some lumber and build a boat," he told Johnson. "I'll drop down river, you prospect these bars."

The back-breaking device called a "whipsaw" helped many a miner during this period of time. It consisted of an open scaffold on which a log was placed. Planks were then cut from a log with a long two-handled saw, one man sawing from below and the other from above.

Once he'd built his boat, Bremner tried a few promising streams with little success. Then one day, about noon, he reached the mouth of Dolby River and stopped for a bite to eat at a Native fish camp where two women, three or four children, a young man and a shaman were fishing.

The old prospector asked the Natives to share his fried duck and tea. After they'd eaten, Bremner put his grub box in the boat and motioned for the men to shove the boat off shore. Bremner had left his gun in the boat close to the bow.

One of the men grabbed the old man's double-barreled gun and fired. Bremner fell, but was not dead, so the other barrel was fired. Bremner's body rolled into the river and was never found.

Some informants said only one of the men had shot Bremner, but another report said the medicine man finished him off. Whatever the details, Bremner was dead.

After sharing his lunch of fried duck and tea with Natives at a fish camp, much like the one pictured above, John Bremner was shot dead while putting his boat back in the water. Note the sheet iron stove in front of "Old Eliza" sitting outside the tent. This type of stove was used extensively by the Indians, trappers and prospectors of the era.

A man named John Minook, part Russian and part Native, brought news of the murder to Nuklukyet, where about 60 prospectors were waiting for steamboats coming up from St. Michael with supplies. Their reactions to the news were swift and angry.

Miners commandeer a steamer

"If it takes all summer, let's go after the murderers and hang them," cried the miners. "We'll have to teach those Indians it isn't safe to kill prospectors."

Law, as represented by police, sheriffs and courts, had not penetrated this part of Alaska in the 1880s. There was only the law of the miners. The prospectors held a meeting and voted to avenge old John, because they were sure he hadn't provoked the attack. John had always gotten along with the Native people.

But first the miners had to have a boat. Knowing that steamers from St. Michael soon would be coming upriver, the men went to the mouth of the Koyukuk to wait. In a few days, they saw smoke downriver. When the boat got closer, they recognized the little river steamer *Explorer*, which belonged to Aneasum Belkof of Russian Mission.

"It's just the boat we need, boys," cried Hank Wright, one of the leaders. "It's for shallow water – come on, let's go aboard!"

A committee of six miners quickly leapt to the deck of the boat as it tied up to the bank. Hank was appointed spokesman.

"Old John Bremner was killed up the Koyukuk by some Indians. We want you to take us up there," he said.

"Can't boys," answered the captain. "I've got freight to haul. I'm not taking my boat up the Koyukuk."

"Don't get excited," the miners, just as determined, told him. "We've got your boat, and if you won't take us, we'll take it ourselves and you and your passengers can get off!"

In spite of Capt. Bordwine's indignation, the passengers were persuaded to disembark, and the two barges of freight tied to the *Explorer* were left tied at the mouth of the Koyukuk.

Miners head off to find killers

Twenty miners and two Natives, Minook and a man named Pitka, who'd been talked into going along as guides and interpreters, trooped onboard the steamer.

The *Explorer* steamed away amid much cheering from those onboard and those left on the bank. The ones on the boat had greased their faces, hands and necks with a mixture of lard and tar as protection against mosquitoes and made quite a fearsome spectacle.

At an organizational meeting, the miners picked Gordon Bettles as captain, with Bill Moore and Jim Bender next in command. Hank Wright was boss of all men on deck.

Soon after their departure, they stopped to cut wood. And with all the good axmen onboard, it didn't take long to fill every available space.

As they turned into the Koyukuk, they passed a high bluff, a landmark visible for many miles called Koyukuk Sopka by the Russians. The land was monotonous with a serpentine channel and densely wooded banks lined with scrubby willow and cottonwood trees.

Miners in a hurry to catch Old John Bremner's killers stopped long enough to cut piles of wood, which they shoved into every available space on the steamer *Explorer* for its trip up the Koyukuk.

Miners seeking justice for Old John Bremner's murder took the steamship *Explorer*, which resembled the one shown in this picture, up the Koyukuk River and then into a shallow stream. They finally came across the village they were looking for, where the miners convinced the villagers to hand over the men that eyewitnesses said killed the old prospector.

The river varied in width from 500 to 1,000 yards, bending to the left, then to the right, and dotted with numerous islands and piles of bleaching driftwood. Minook thought it would take several days to get to the Indian camp from the mouth of the river, but the miners intended to make a quick trip of it.

"We'll get all we can out of the boat," said the captain. "If it can't stand it, it can go to the bottom!"

It stood the river, however. The firemen, stripped to their waists and with sweat running down their backs, pushed wood as fast as they could, but it was four days before they came to the mouth of the Dolby.

Miners find suspects

There the miners saw a cache of drying fish, some of Bremner's tools and the old prospector's boat, all torn up. Two Native women and some children fishing along the bank told the miners that the suspects had headed upstream.

"Get up steam," ordered the captain. "And keep out of sight."

The miners posted lookouts, one on each side of the pilot house, while the rest of the men hid below decks. The boat slowly steamed up the stream, which was so narrow that the sides of the vessel scraped the banks. Soon the lookouts spotted smoke ahead and the men made ready to jump ashore.

The *Explorer* was the first steamboat to navigate the Koyukuk, and the sight of the smoke-belching apparition frightened the 80 villagers so much that the prospectors were able to surround them in a flash. Two men tried to run away, but they were quickly captured.

John Minook, shown here with his family in Rampart, told the miners of John Bremner's murder and then accompanied them on their steamboat ride to capture Bremner's killers. Minook later made a discovery of gold along the Yukon that established the boomtown of Rampart.

Minook questioned the chief as to who killed the white prospector. The villagers then turned over the two men who had tried to escape, a young man named Silas and his uncle, Treneneon.

"We are going to hang these men," the miners told the villagers. "And if your people kill any more whites, we'll come back and take the murders and their families and hang them all."

Miners' justice

With their prisoners in custody, the miners boarded their boat and backed down the stream a half-mile before they could turn around. They then made quick time to the mouth of the river where they stopped and held a trial.

The miners had Minook ask the Native men which one killed the old prospector.

"I did," said the younger man, but some of the judges thought he seemed more afraid of the medicine man than of being hanged and so said, "They're both guilty."

Others thought that only the young man should be punished because he confessed. To settle the dispute, the men drew a line in the sand.

"Those who think that both should hang step over the line," said the spokesman.

Only seven stepped over, so only one noose was prepared. But before the miners hung the young man on a cottonwood tree, they asked him why he'd shot the old man.

"I wanted the white man's gun, blanket and tobacco," he replied, according to some of the witnesses.

Perhaps the wrong man was punished, however, for others have said the shaman instigated the killing because he and other shamans foresaw the whites overtaking Native country and wanted to stop that from happening.

After the medicine man returned to his village, the young Native man's family tried to kill him. An intertribal feud then went on for years between the families of the two men, which resulted in several more deaths.

The miners sincerely believed they had done their duty and had executed old John's murderer. They stopped at every Native camp on their way back to return the *Explorer* to its owner to tell the people what they had done and why.

And although Bremner died without finding the mother lode of gold that had beckoned him, he did not sink into anonymity as befell so many unsuccessful prospectors. Bremner River, John River and Old John Lake will forever remind us of old John Bremner.

But Bremner wasn't the only early prospector who searched for gold in the Koyukuk area. Nor was he the only one to have places named after him.

15

RICH NAMES ALONG THE KOYUKUK

Long before the Klondike gold rush, evidence of prospectors plying the waters of the Koyukuk River, seen here in 1899, were found in rusty fragments of iron implements and weathered ax marks on trees.

Above, a steamer pushes a barge loaded with supplies up the Yukon River circa 1900.

Even though Lt. Henry Allen thought he was the first white man to penetrate so far up the Koyukuk, pioneer prospectors came before him, if traditions among old-timers are correct. Hudson Stuck says there are very few parts of the Interior that were not visited by prospectors.

Below, miners take off with pack trains from an Interior Alaska village in search of their fortunes around 1898.

The Koyukuk – land of turbulence, gold and mighty men of magic. There is evidence of a rich heritage in the names of historic villages along the river – names such as Batzna, Moses Village, Allakaket, Nok, Kakliaklia, Wiseman, Bergman, Hughes, Bettles – Native villages and gold rush towns.

Few white men had visited the Koyukuk region until John Bremner showed up in the mid-1880s. The Russians were the first on the Yukon River, in 1834, but they weren't looking for gold; furs were a much richer treasure.

But even in those early days, rumors that gold existed in then-Russian America managed to reach the ears of Alexander Baranof, "the rum-swilling Lord of Alaska, who ruled the peninsula from the island bastion of Sitka," according to Pierre Berton in "The Klondike Fever."

"But Baranov (Baranof), garnering a fortune in furs for his Czarist masters against an incongruous background of fine books, costly paintings, and brilliantly plumaged officers and women, was not anxious for a gold rush. When one of the Russians babbled drunkenly of gold, so legend has it, the Lord of Alaska ordered him shot."

Lt. Henry Allen arrived in 1885 to explore the area. He traveled the Copper, Tanana and Yukon rivers, and leaving the Yukon a few miles below Tanana, pursued the ridge between the Tozitna and Melozitna rivers, passing a tributary of the Kornutna and arriving at the upper Koyukuk; he had made the journey from Tanana to Kornuchaket in 6-1/2 days.

By canoe, Allen went as far up the river as the present town of Bettles, mapping the river's course and naming several islands, then he drifted back down to the river's mouth. He named Higgens Island, for instance, after a brigadier general of the U. S. Army thrice wounded at Chickamunga.

Evidence of early prospectors

Even though Allen thought he was the first white man to penetrate so far up the Koyukuk, pioneer prospectors were before him, if

Many miners panned for gold along the Koyukuk River during the 1880s and some left their names as evidence of their existence, including Wiseman, Bettles and Bergman.

traditions among old-timers are correct. Hughes Bar, they said, was named for a man who came up the river a year before Allen.

John Hughes was a former New York City policeman. Why he left New York to seek gold in the North was never disclosed, but Hudson Stuck says in his book, "Voyages on the Yukon and Its Tributaries," that Hughes City, which dates from 1910, should have been named for John Hughes instead of for the then-governor of New York.

It may safely be said, according to Stuck, that there are very few parts of the Interior that were not visited by prospectors. They made no maps and left no records, and only now and then does evidence of their visits crop up.

Old prospectors tell of reaching some remote creek into which they think they are the first to visit, and perhaps a rusty fragment of iron implement, an almost obliterated yet quite unmistakable disturbance of the surface, or weathered ax mark upon a tree, bear conclusive evidence that someone else was there before. In the Indian River camp behind Hughes City, the miners say they found signs of earlier workings, quite forgotten even by miners' tradition.

Gold camps spring up

The gold-rush period of Koyukuk history was a turbulent and interesting one. Gold was discovered on Evans Bar, Tramway Bar and on Hughes Bar in 1890, according to Gordon Bettles, pioneer of the Koyukuk country.

Bettles told how he started his "bean shops," as he called his trading posts, in an article in a 1941 issue of *Alaska Life*. The first he established at Arctic City in 1894. The next one he built at Bergman, which often flooded out. That's when Bettles opened another post and named it after himself.

A constant procession of river steamers chugged up the Yukon and then headed up the Koyukuk, all loaded down with stampeders and their supplies, Bettles said. Once, 68 steamers were frozen in solid for the long, cold winter when a sudden cold spell took them unawares. There were 900 people on those ships, and when the adventurers realized they would have to remain a whole year in this desolate part of Alaska, 550 of them took emergency rations and mushed out to the Yukon.

Many went downstream to St. Michael, vowing never again to visit such an inhospitable country, but 350 stampeders stayed in and around Bettles.

"We had quite an interesting winter with such a varied assortment," Bettles said.

Mastodon graveyard reported

Between 1899 and 1901, the Revenue Cutter *Nunivak* was on duty along the Yukon, enforcing custom and navigation laws. One of its officers, Second Lt. B.H. Camden, made a reconnaissance of the Koyukuk River and wrote in his report, titled "Report of the Operations of the U.S. Steamer Nunivak on the Yukon River Station, Alaska, 1899-1901," that one of the most noticeable features of the

Second Lt. B.H. Camden, traveling along the Koyukuk River between 1899 and 1901, noted a glacial formation that seemed to be the graveyard of several mastodons.

Many stampeders with dreams of gold got as far as Slate Creek, then got cold feet and turned back. Sources say that's how the settlement of Coldfoot, pictured here beyond the trees in the early 1900s, got its name.

Koyukuk was in the formation of its bars, which were composed of gravel, not sand as along the Yukon.

Camden also mentioned Mastodon Bank, a glacial formation that seemed to be the graveyard of mastodons, for many teeth and bones belonging to that animal had been found there.

"It is probably that a herd of mastodons were overtaken by some disaster, the remains being preserved in ice and the carcasses only exposed from time to time by the current cutting into the bank during unusually high water," Camden wrote.

At the time he made his reconnaissance, the total Native population was not more than 300, and fishing in the summer and hunting and trapping in the winter was their chief occupation and means of subsistence.

He also observed that the now-elevated channel once formed the bed of a river, changed by some upheaval of the earth, and from its general direction, Camden believed it to have flowed into the Bering Sea near Nome.

First streams to yield gold

The first streams on the Koyukuk to yield gold in large quantities were Myrtle, Emma and Gold creeks, and as early as 1899, the town of Slate Creek was started. In the summer of 1900, one of the waves of green stampeders got as far as this point, then got cold feet, turned back and left – reason enough to change the name of the settlement to Coldfoot.

Wiseman was named after a transient prospector who stopped a few minutes to pan gold at the mouth of Wiseman Creek and perpetuated his name. Bergman was named for a steamboat captain.

Whenever a steamboat tied up, a few cabins were built on the bank. An official from the Land Office was onboard a boat, and he laid out a town site at one point, with a church, school and courthouse, First and Second avenues, all neatly laid out on paper. It was named

Prospectors in the Koyukuk country eventually found rich deposits of gold. By the spring of 1908, there were hundreds of men working the diggings.

Peavy, and on blueprint looked quite impressive. When the official returned to Washington, he carried the name and locations of these settlements, and although they had only a year or so of existence, their names dotted the maps of the upper Koyukuk — Seaforth, Union City, Jimtown, Beaver City, Arctic City and Peavy. They were taken off later editions of government maps.

There was excitement, activity and violence during this mining period, including the murder of old John Bremner, one of the earliest prospectors who left his name on the John River, a tributary of the Koyukuk. Hudson Stuck thought that his murder was instigated by medicine men who could foresee the result of prospectors coming into the country.

The Blueberry Kid

Another violent chapter in the history of the Koyukuk was written on the lower reaches of the river in the fall of 1912.

"The 'Blueberry Kid' was thought to have murdered 'Fiddler John' (the discoverer of gold on the Hammond River), 'Dutch Marie,' a notorious woman from Nolan, both going outside with 'home stakes' from their respective occupations, and Frank Adams, whose death was necessary to the robbery and murder of the others," wrote Stuck.

"The last steamboat was gone from Bettles, so the Blueberry Kid took the aforementioned as passengers on his launch, the miner and the woman both drunk when they embarked. The Kid alone reached Nulato, took a steamboat to St. Michael and so 'outside,' and in Seattle it is said cashed thousands of dollars worth of gold dust at the Mint, and again in San Francisco.

"The launch was found two years later, swamped in a backwater but still tied to a tree. (Witnesses said) the Blueberry Kid had arrived at Nulato in a collapsible canvas boat he carried in the launch. Two years later, somebody found a little heap of calcined bones at an old campsite near the submerged launch, but I do not think that any effort was made to determine if they were human remains or not, and the Blueberry Kid is still at large."

Loads of gold leave the Koyukuk

The Alaska Commercial Company bought Bettles' "bean shop" at Bettles, and in 1902, Volney Richmond was assigned to the growing store. In the fall of 1903, he made the largest gold shipment ever sent out of Bettles, $250,000. The Koyukuk's biggest year was in 1909 when $420,000 worth of gold was taken out of the diggings. Although there was still a great amount of gold being taken out of the ground after 1903, the number of people along the river declined. In 1906, there was a big stampede into the adjacent Chandalar country, which depleted the Koyukuk ranks to the point that in two years its population was cut in half.

However, in the autumn of 1907, Swedes John and Louis Olson and John Anderson were given a strip of ground 300 feet wide on Nolan Creek, and here they found almost unbelievable fortune. The three took out $100,000 the first winter and in three years recovered $250,000.

New gold rushes along the Koyukuk

By the spring of 1908, there were more than 200 new men rushing into the Koyukuk. And just as the riches of Nolan Creek commenced to wane, the deep channel of Hammond River was located in the spring of 1911. During the next five years, more than $1 million came out of this valley.

The peak year of Koyukuk's second boom came in 1915 when more than 400 tons of freight was brought in for the 300 Caucasians and perhaps 75 Natives living in the region. By 1916, however, the richest claims both of Nolan Creek and Hammond River were mined, and the high wages of World War I convinced many of the most energetic men to leave. Its heyday was over, and mining was never so important again.

In Merle Colby's "Guide to Alaska," the author says that for the sheer joy of finding gold, perhaps no other district has as much lure as does the Koyukuk region, for much of the gold there is very coarse. The big money has been pretty well mined out, but if anyone would like to try his luck at prospecting, "here is the place to do it!"

But the Koyukuk wasn't the only place in Alaska that was yielding gold during the 1880s. Prospectors were trickling into the Kenai Peninsula, as well, and it wasn't long before thousands more would flood into places like Sunrise and Hope, searching for rocks that glittered.

16

ALASKA'S SECOND GOLD RUSH

A few years after the rush into Southeast Alaska, and just before the famed gold rush of the Klondike, prospectors streamed into another part of Alaska in search of riches beyond their wildest imaginations. Creeks on the Kenai Peninsula beckoned miners to test their muscle and fortitude after some promising deposits were located around Resurrection and Sixmile creeks.

Although Russians first set foot in Alaska in 1741, few official records exist before the Russian-American Company was formed to show they had any formal expeditions to search for precious metals around the Kenai area.

Russian interest in the possibilities of gold deposits in Alaska surfaced after the 1848 discovery of gold in California. In 1849, the Russian-America Company sent mining engineer Peter Doroshin to the Kenai area to search for gold.

The graduate of the Imperial Mining School at St. Petersburg arrived in Cook Inlet too late to thoroughly explore for the metal, although he did find traces of gold to pique his interest. The following year, he prospected and found colors all around the mouth of the Kenai River. That year and the next he headed farther up the river and found even larger gold grains.

His discoveries must not have held much merit with the company, however, for it pulled him off his search for gold in 1852 and instructed him to look for coal instead. But even though his mining venture didn't prove as fruitful as the company had hoped, Doroshin was convinced that large placer gold deposits were hidden in the Kenai Mountains.

This appears to be the only recorded official gold-hunting expedition made by the Russian-American Company, according to Mary J. Barry in her book, "A History of Mining on the Kenai Peninsula, Alaska."

"However, American prospectors attest to finding numerous Russian mining artifacts at several locations on the Kenai Peninsula," Barry wrote, which indicates that the Russians did more prospecting. "Square-shaped Russian nails and other metal items were found on the Mathison placer properties on Resurrection Creek. Russian artifacts were found at the base of Slaughter Gulch and Devil's Gulch.

American prospectors attest to finding numerous Russian mining artifacts at several locations on the Kenai Peninsula. Russians, who arrived in the mid-1700s and established their settlements, built the Russian Orthodox Church of the Dormition, above, in Kenai in 1846.

A few prospectors were finding their way into the Cook Inlet region of Alaska during the 1880s. Gold-seekers often had to float their sleds across rivers with horses guiding the way.

While prospecting on Bear Creek near Hope in 1893, George Beady, F.R. Walcott and Patrick Reilly claimed to find evidences of Russian mining."

Russians mum about gold discoveries

Some historians speculate that the Russian government knew there were gold deposits in Alaska, but it didn't broadcast the fact because it feared a rush of gold-seeking Americans or British into its colonies.

A few decades later, prospectors proved that hunch correct.

Around 1888, a prospector named Alexander King arrived at Kenai and convinced Capt. Charles Swanson, who owned a trading post, to grubstake him for two summers and a winter. A grubstake usually consisted of enough food and supplies to keep a man for one season and was valued at around $500.

After loading his grubstake into his old dory, King jumped in his boat and rowed up Turnagain Arm.

"The people of Cook Inlet called the Arm the 'Cannonball' for the swiftness of the tides," Barry wrote. "No prospector, as far as is known, had rowed up that way previously, as the going was almost impossibly difficult with oars alone, and no one had gas engines those days."

Late in the second summer King reappeared in Kenai with four pokes of gold. He paid off his grubstake debt and resumed his search for the mother lode. Five years later, in 1893, he staked the Alex King claim at Resurrection Creek.

Word of King's discovery, as well as discoveries on Mills Creek and Sixmile Creek near Girdwood, trickled down to the California mining camps. Soon streams of prospectors were making their way north. In May 1895, one prospector named Hans Siverson wrote to

Prospecting parties settled into the Turnagain Arm, Hope District, in the 1890s in hopes of finding the fortunes that had so far eluded them. This prospecting party is settling in at Spruce Camp at the head of Turnagain Arm.

By 1896, thousands of prospectors had flocked to Cook Inlet looking for the mother lode of gold. Hope, above, and Sunrise, below, both pictured in 1906, served as supply and entertainment centers for miners along Resurrection Creek and Turnagain Arm.

his friends about the conditions in Turnagain Arm that appeared in the Alaska Mining Record.

"I landed at Turnagain Arm a few days ago and found everything as I expected it to be. The diggings so far discovered are not very extensive, nor are they so very rich. The Bear Creek or Beede's diggings are good for five or six dollars to the man, but do not appear to be lasting. There is one thing that must be born (sic) in mind; the country has not been prospected to any extent. Bob Michaelson, Bill Williams, John Rainey (Renner), Trapp and others have been on Resurrection Creek for four or five years and have scarcely made a living mining fine gold, and Bear Creek with plenty of coarse gold was but two miles away. The reason of that is they came here broke and had to get in and dig for their living at once.

"I would not advise anyone to come here with the expectation of finding anything fabulously rich, although a man can make a

Prospectors had to whipsaw lumber to make sluice boxes and build cabins in the Cook Inlet area. The back-breaking task took two men to slice through logs to make planks.

good living anywhere here with a rocker. The old timers here have good faith in the country and say all that it needs is prospecting. In fact, colors can be found on almost every shovel full of gravel on the creeks. ..."

Second gold rush takes off

By 1896, Alaska's second gold rush was in full swing. Articles in large newspapers like The San Francisco Chronicle and The New York Times drew about 3,000 prospectors to Cook Inlet. After landing at Tyonek, the regular stop for Alaska Commercial steamships, some miners went up the Susitna River while others traveled up Turnagain Arm in smaller vessels that transported people and supplies in shallower waters.

The first arrivals were seasoned miners from other parts of Alaska, Canada and the West Coast. The inexperienced, filled with grand dreams of easy riches, followed.

Settlements like Hope, which some say was named after 17-year-old prospector Percy Hope, and Sunrise sprang up along the shores of Turnagain Arm. By July 1896, Sunrise had several stores, a brewery, two saloons and two restaurants where meals cost 50 cents, according to Barry.

Mining was simple. The liberal use of a pick and shovel, as well as a strong back, was all that most men needed. Miners shoveled gravel from gold-bearing streams into long, narrow, wooden boxes called sluices. The miners then ran water over the gravel and slats, which were laid crosswise in the bottom of the boxes, caught the gold and the gravel waste, called tailings, washed through.

Hydraulic mining came later. A high-pressure water jet was used to break up the gravel, which then was washed through a sluice box. A lot of gravel could be run through in a short amount of time, which meant that lower-grade gravel could be mined for a profit.

Miners dug long ditches on hillsides above their claims to collect water and funnel it down to the mining area so they had enough water pressure to wash the gravel.

"The men who located property and wintered at Sunrise and

Hope made good wages for that time – about $4 to $6 a day per man, on the average," Barry wrote. "The Alaska Mining Record, summarizing the business of 1896, estimated Cook Inlet placer mine production at $175,000."

Cook Inlet rush ends

The Cook Inlet rush ended about as abruptly as it started. By the spring of 1897, hundreds of people had left the area. The best sites had already been claimed along the gold belt and small workforces could mine those claims.

Although another rush of people poured into the area in 1898, and made Sunrise the largest city in Alaska for a short time, most left after efficient hydraulic mining equipment arrived that drove out the small prospectors.

And whatever happened to that prospector who first paddled his way up the Turnagain Arm?

Sunrise became the largest city in Alaska for a short time during a second rush to Cook Inlet in 1898.

King's luck didn't hold, according to Barry. He left the Kenai Peninsula and headed to the Yukon River in the summer of 1900. While working on a river freighter for a man named Herbert Davenport, white-bearded King got upset when the scow kept getting grounded on sandbars.

The short, thickset man flew into a rage on the evening of July 18 when the boat again became stuck and he shot Davenport in the heart.

Shipmates, fearing for their own lives, agreed to tell authorities it was an accidental shooting and convinced King to keep Davenport's body onboard to lessen suspicion.

However, when the freighter pulled into Dawson, the crew members told the truth and King was arrested. He confessed to the killing and was hung by the Royal Canadian Mounted Police on Oct. 2, 1900.

Just as King's Cook Inlet rush was coming to an end, another was just beginning along tributaries of the Yukon River following another prospector's major discovery.

17

DREAMS OF SALMON TURN TO GOLD
Christmas Thoughts
Christmas Eve, 1888

I am camped on a mountainside tonight,
one hundred miles from the sea,
And the smell of the caribou steak on the coals,
is a grateful odor to me
For the deer were fleet-footed and shy today,
and I've roamed the mountain's breast,
'Till the bearskin robe on my cozy bed
seems beckoning me to rest.
But a tall, old spruce by the campfire's glow
bows his glittering top to me,
And seems to whisper, " 'Tis Christmas Eve,
and I'm your Christmas tree."
Then a flood of memories o'er me creep
and my spirit afar doth roam,
To where there's another glittering tree,
in a California home.
There all is light and life and love,
and the children laugh with glee,
And I cannot but wonder, with wistful pain,
are they thinking tonight of me?
But a whisper comes from the tall, old spruce,
and my soul from pain is free,
For I know when they kneel together tonight,
they'll all be praying for me.

These lines, found in an old memorandum book, were written by a man who wandered up and down the Yukon River for 11 years before his gold discovery electrified the world. Over glaciers, through marshes, among forests, lakes, rivers and mountains, George Washington Carmack traveled with his Native companions. He seemed a misfit in a land where every man was searching for gold. He only wanted to live like the Natives among whom he'd made his home since coming north in 1885.

Yet, it was he and his trusted Native friends, Skookum Jim and Tagish Charley, who discovered gold on a creek that old-time prospectors dismissed as "too wide and too deep and besides the willows don't lean right."

George Washington Carmack's friend Tagish Charley and his dogs haul a sled loaded with supplies to Tagish, Yukon Territory. Tagish Charley, also known as Káa Goox and Dawson Charley, was a cousin of Carmack's wife, Kate, and part of the famous discovery of gold along the Klondike.

While gold-seekers were scrambling and digging for the precious metal from Birch Creek to Fortymile, indolent, easy-going Carmack went up and down the Yukon fishing, hunting and living off the land. No one took him seriously – the men at Fortymile called him "Lying George," for he always tried to present his fortunes in the best favorable light.

Unlike hard-working prospectors, George had time for the "better things of life." In his cabin he had an organ and a library, including such journals as *Scientific American* and *Review of Reviews*. He enjoyed talking on scientific matters and writing sentimental poetry like his "Christmas Thoughts."

Carmack has "frontier spirit"

Born at Port Costa, Calif., George had grown up in that California home he dreamed about one Christmas in the far North Country. He came from an old frontier family, for his father had been one of the

"Forty-Niners" who came West in a covered wagon to search for gold in California. George, born Sept. 24, 1869, had the frontier spirit, too, and the unexplored reaches of Alaska and the Northwest drew him.

He shipped to Alaska onboard *The Queen of the Pacific*, leaving San Francisco on March 31, 1885, and transferred to the steamer *Idaho* in Port Townsend, Wash. He disembarked at Juneau, signed in at a hotel and soon met two brothers, Hugh and Albert Day, who had prospected in the Yukon and were on their way back to dig for gold again.

Carmack talked three other adventurers into joining him, and they struck out on May 16, 1885, to seek their fortunes in the Yukon. But by August, he had returned

George Washington Carmack, credited with starting the gold rush to the Klondike, at first thought his dream of fish with gold nuggets for scales meant that he should go fishing.

to the Southeast town. Between 1885 and 1896, he wandered back and forth from the Arctic coast to the Pacific coast and worked as a packer over the Chilkoot Pass.

Carmack joined Maj. William Ogilvie's survey party, sent to survey the Alaska-Canada boundary in 1887. He guided the party over the pass to Lake Bennett, for by this time, Carmack knew the country well and could speak both the Chilkoot, or Tlingit, and Tagish, or Tenneh, languages and was very helpful to Ogilvie in dealing with the Indians. George truly enjoyed being among Alaska's Native people.

Carmack enjoys Native way of life

In fact, it was said that one couldn't please him better than to tell him he was "getting to be more and more like an Indian every day." Jowly, round-faced Carmack married the Tagish chief's daughter. When she died soon after their marriage, Carmack married her sister, Kate (Shaaw Tláa). Many said his ambition was to become chief of the tribe.

James Mason (Keish), above, and Tagish Charley (Káa Goox), left, befriended George Washington Carmack and were co-discoverers of the Klondike gold fields.

His two inseparable friends, Kate's brother James Mason (Keish), who everyone called Skookum Jim, and their nephew, Tagish Charley (Káa Goox), also called Dawson Charley, packed occasionally and did odd jobs for trader John Healy at Dyea.

Carmack also made an effort to do something with the coal he'd discovered near the settlement known now as Carmack's, Yukon Territory. He grew tired of the effort, however, and in 1895 posted a note on his cabin door that read, "Gone to Fortymile for grub," and never returned.

He and his Indian friends secured an outfit at Fort Selkirk and passed the winter instead. He was alone, however, when in the spring of 1896, while sitting one day among the ruins of old Fort Selkirk, he had a premonition as he gazed on the morning state – a premonition that a great change was coming into his life.

Carmack's premonition

"Right then and there," he later recalled, "I made up my mind to take action on that hunch, so taking a silver dollar out of my pocket – that was all the cheechako money I had – I flipped it high into the air."

While sitting among the ruins of old Fort Selkirk on the Yukon River in the spring of 1896, George Washington Carmack had a premonition that a change was coming into his life. Shortly thereafter, he made a discovery that brought thousands of people to the Klondike.

If it came up heads, he thought it meant he should go upstream. If tails, it meant that fate had something in store for him downstream. Tails turned up, so Carmack got into his canoe and started paddling downstream the 200 miles or so to Fortymile.

His mystic experience wasn't finished, however, for that night he had a vivid dream.

"I dreamed that I was sitting on the bank of a small stream of water, watching the grayling shoot the rapids. Suddenly, the grayling began to scatter as two large king salmon shot up the stream in a flurry of foaming water and came to a dead stop in front of the bank where I was sitting.

"They were two beautiful fish, but I noticed that instead of having scales like salmon, they were covered with an armor of bright, gold nuggets and had $20 gold pieces for eyes. ..."

Like George W. Carmack, many miners traveled to Fortymile, shown above, to restock supplies and share information while searching for gold along the Klondike.

Carmack goes fishing

How he reacted to the dream casts some insight into Carmack's character, for he took this dream as a sign, not that he should hunt for gold, but that he should go fishing.

But fish where? After careful thought, he decided upon the Throndiuk – later called Klondike – because it was a good salmon stream. And so it was that the riches of the Klondike were discovered.

On the first of July 1896, he left Fortymile for his fishing expedition and was joined by his wife, Kate, at least one of his children, whom miners called "Graphie Gracey" because they couldn't pronounce her Indian name, and of course, Jim and Charley.

The men set their nets and hauled in a few king salmon, but the fishing was very poor – the poorest Carmack could remember.

The men gave up fishing and cut timber instead. The sawmill at Fortymile paid $25 per 1,000 board feet, and the men saw it as a chance to make a few dollars before winter.

Jim went in search of some good lumber about a mile up the Klondike. He turned south and followed a stream called Rabbit Creek.

Skookum Jim finds flecks

Jim found a sturdy stand of trees and closely examined the water to see if logs could be floated downstream. He saw some flecks of gold and reported it to Carmack. But neither Carmack nor Charley showed any interest.

Earlier that July they'd been approached by a white man, Robert Henderson, who told Carmack that he'd found prospects on some little creeks that drained into the Klondike – about 15 miles up from Carmack's camp.

When Carmack asked about the chances of locating there, the Nova Scotian glanced toward Jim and Charley, and said with an air of scorn, "Well, there's a chance for you, George, but I don't want any damn Siwashes staking on that creek."

This is a view of Bonanza Creek Valley from across the Klondike River.

Threesome travels down Rabbit Creek

His remark rankled Skookum Jim.

"Never mind, Jim," Carmack told his friend. "This is a big country; we'll find a creek of our own."

Carmack's restless nature, however, prompted him to take a look at Henderson's diggings, but because of the presence of Jim and Charley, they were received coolly.

Exactly what happened next has been disputed, but two facts are clear. First, Carmack promised Henderson that if he found anything worthwhile on Rabbit Creek he would send word back. Second, Carmack's friends tried to buy some tobacco from Henderson, but the white man refused to sell to them. He might have been short of supplies, but it is more likely that he refused because of his dislike of Indians. That attitude was to cost him dearly.

Carmack and his friends were not impressed with the prospects at Henderson's diggings, anyway, and they started back over the mountains almost at once. It was hard going. Fallen trees and devil's clubs barred their path.

They had to force their way through underbrush, flounder over spongy tundra and hop from clump to clump. Gnats and mosquitoes aggravated them, but they had to let the insects feast, for if they swatted the pesky bugs, they'd lose their footing and sink into the glacial ooze.

There are many stories as to the actual finding of gold on Rabbit Creek. But Maj. William Ogilvie obtained a true and accurate account, which he wrote in his book, "Early Days on the Yukon." Ogilvie interviewed Carmack, Charley and Jim separately and together to discuss, criticize and reconcile their stories.

The men had exhausted their provisions before they got very far down the creek. Their progress was slow due to prospecting along the way, and at last they were too tired and weak to go any farther. Jim went hunting, shot a moose, and called for the others, who were a short distance away, to come to him.

After George W. Carmack, Skookum Jim and Tagish Charley discovered gold along Rabbit Creek, they renamed their find "Bonanza" and built sluice boxes to sift out the gold.

The cabin in the foreground is where George Carmack and his friends discovered the first major gold deposit in the Klondike. Bonanza Creek and Gold Hill are seen to the right. The mouth of Eldorado Creek is just beyond Gold Hill.

Jim spies gold-filled sand

While waiting for his friends to join him, Jim looked at the sand of the creek where he'd gone to get a drink. He found gold, he said, in greater quantities than he had ever seen before. That was Aug. 17, 1896, a memorable day that still is celebrated in the Yukon Territory.

The three men spent two days at this place, panning and testing the gravel up and down the creek, and they satisfied themselves that they had the best spot. Deciding to stake and record there, they got into a dispute as to who should stake the Discovery Claim.

In mining terms, the Discovery Claim was the first claim in a region and the center point of a mining district. The claims upstream from the Discovery Claim were numbered "One Above," and the claims downstream were called "One Below" and so on. Preceding the number was the name of the creek on which the claim was found.

Skookum Jim thought the Discovery Claim on Rabbit Creek

should be his by right of discovery, but Carmack told him that an Indian would not be allowed to record it. They finally decided the question by Carmack staking the Discovery Claim and assigning a half-interest in it to Jim. Since the discoverer was entitled to a second claim, Carmack staked number One Below Discovery, too, and number Two Below was staked for Tagish Charley, while Skookum Jim staked number One Above.

Since they felt they had found a bonanza, they decided to rename Rabbit Creek and called it Bonanza. They panned out enough gold to fill a Winchester rifle cartridge shell, and the party then proceeded to the mouth of the Yukon. There they had prepared a raft of saw logs for the mill at Fortymile and on it Carmack and Charley went down to record the claims. Jim was sent back to cut timber for sluice boxes and keep an eye on the claims, for the country around was alive with claim jumpers looking for Henderson's discovery.

Carmack's discovery of gold along Rabbit Creek started the gold rush that brought thousands of hopeful miners to the Klondike in 1897-1898. Skookum Jim, middle, is seen here at Discovery Claim on Bonanza Creek.

Carmack shares news of discovery

Henderson always bitterly resented Carmack's neglect to send him word of the new discovery, as Henderson said Carmack had promised. He did not learn of the new discovery until after all the rich ground was staked. Carmack seemed to have made no effort to let Henderson in on it, although he might have if Henderson had not insulted Jim and Charley, and by implication, himself.

Not much attention was paid to Carmack and Tagish Charley when they reached Fortymile and told about the new discovery. Carmack first stopped off at Bill McPhee's saloon on his way to the mining recorder's office. He felt, he remembered later, "as if I had just dealt myself a royal flush in the game of life," and he wanted to deal in the men of Fortymile as well. He felt he was on the threshold of fame, respect and admiration.

When responses to his announcement were derisive and disbelieving, he pulled out the cartridge shell full of gold and dropped it on the bar. Gold of each creek is characteristic of that creek alone, so when the experienced miners examined Carmack's sample, they saw it was different from any they had ever seen. All skepticism vanished, as they knew Carmack had found a new gold-bearing stream.

The rush is on

GOLD! The rush was on. Drunken men were thrown into boats. One man was tied and made to go along. By midnight, the stampede was in full swing and Fortymile was deserted in just a few hours. Two hundred claims were staked before the news got down to Oscar Ashby's saloon in Circle City.

At first, Carmack, Charley and Jim worked together on Discovery One Above and One and Two Below. That is, Charley was supposed to be helping, but actually Jim did most of the work.

In the spring of 1897, the men sold half of Tagish Charley's Two Below and received $13,750. Charley and Jim put up a sluice box over the remaining ground and washed gold when they were in the mood. They had to carry the dirt to the sluices in the same clumsy boxes in which they hauled the dirt from the shaft.

But after their winter paydirt dumps were sluiced out in spring 1898, Carmack and his friends received their first big payout. The three men divided about $150,000 once they'd paid off the men who'd worked for them and paid all the required royalties to the Canadian government. The group then leased out their claims and Carmack, Kate, Jim and Charley went down to Seattle to see what civilization had to offer.

Seeing the sights of Seattle

They stayed in the Butler, one of the best hotels in town. But the hotel had so many floors, halls and stairways that Kate used her skinning knife to slash a series of blazes on doors and mahogany banisters to keep from getting lost on the trail from the Carmack suite to the dining room.

Klondikers worked feverishly along Bonanza Creek during wintertime mining operations.

After working the rich diggings of their Discovery Claim on Bonanza Creek, George, Kate and Graphie Gracey traveled to Seattle to see what the cosmopolitan city had to offer in the spring of 1897.

She, Jim and Charley acquired a taste for champagne and amused themselves by flinging bills and gold nuggets into the streets. They watched with amusement as crowds pushed and shoved, bringing traffic to a standstill. Several times they were arrested and fined for drunkenness.

Meanwhile, Carmack, now 38, rode up and down the streets with an expensive cigar in his mouth and a sign emblazoned on his carriage identifying him as "George Carmack, Discoverer of Gold in the Yukon."

The merry band of miners returned to the spring cleanup on Bonanza in April 1899. Carmack and his partners divided gold worth close to $200,000 for their efforts, and then returned to Seattle that July, according to James Albert Johnson, author of "George Carmack."

Tagish Charley, Skookum Jim and their families checked into the Seattle Hotel, and the Carmacks stayed at the Brunswick.

Kate makes the news

While Carmack was away inspecting a real-estate investment, Kate and her brother made news for The Seattle Post-Intelligencer:

"Mrs. George W. Carmack, the Indian wife of the discoverer of the Klondike, slept last night in the city jail, charged with being drunk and disorderly and disturbing the peace of the city of Seattle. Under the same roof in the men's ward Skookum Jim, her brother, found lodgings as a plain drunk. So much for the debasing tendencies of great wealth and the firewater of the white man.

"George W. Carmack, whose wife was arrested while executing an aboriginal Yukon war dance in the second floor corridor of the Seattle Hotel yesterday evening at about 6 o'clock, has a fortune estimated at not less than $200,000 in cash and is, besides, the owner of one of the most valuable claims in the Klondike mining district. ..."

Kate Carmack, posing here for a portrait picture in the late 1890s, made Seattle news when she went on a drinking spree.

Tagish Charley made the news a few days later.

Tagish Charley's turn

"The troubles of George Carmack's Indian brothers-in-law are never-ending. Yesterday it was Tagish Charley's turn. After the incarceration of his brother, Skookum Jim, and his sister, Mrs. Carmack, on Tuesday night for drunkenness, Charley continued his uninterrupted spree in company with several white men of more or less shady reputation."

The article said that Tagish Charley had been rebuked for his riotous conduct in the Seattle Hotel Bar and been advised by Seattle Police Sgt. Ward to go home. Later that day, Charley went to the police headquarters and claimed that he'd been taken to the headquarters the previous night and been robbed of gold nugget watches, rings, chains, scarf pins and a diamond stud worth about $400 cash.

"An investigation was made with the result that Tagish Charley's belongings were found in the safe at the Seattle Hotel where he had been induced to leave them at 7 o'clock yesterday morning ... The police say Charley would have been a ripe plum for some highwayman had he strayed away from the hotel before he deposited his valuables with the night clerk."

Carmack was furious with their behavior, wrote Johnson, who found letters written by Carmack to his sister, Rose, in a book store in Seattle. Carmack eventually dissolved his partnerships with Charley and Jim and left Kate because he could not tolerate their drinking any longer.

And civilization and the means to satisfy his desires seemed to have extinguished his wish to live like a Native, which had been his dream before his gold discovery.

Skookum Jim and Tagish Charley stayed at the Seattle Hotel during their foray into civilization.

He met Marguerite Laimee, who owned a cigar store in Dawson, and after a rapid courtship, married her on Oct. 30, 1900.

Gold doesn't bring Kate happiness

Kate was left to live unhappily in the civilized world, and continued to find herself going to jail in the company of one of her relatives. She was staying with Carmack's sister, Rose, when, in 1900, Carmack wrote and said she should be sent North.

She returned to the Yukon in the summer of 1901, where she lived in a cabin built for her by her brother, Jim, who also supported her. Her daughter, Graphie Gracey, attended the mission school begun by Bishop William Carpenter Bompas at Caribou Crossing. Graphie Gracey later went to school in Whitehorse, her tuition paid for by Jim.

Kate finished out her life at Caribou Crossing, later renamed Carcross, on Lake Tagish. As a reminder of better days, she always wore a necklace of nuggets taken from the famous claim on Bonanza Creek. She died in 1920, and an old gray stone marks her grave.

Kate Carmack, pictured here in 1919, lived out her days in Carcross.

Carmack and Marguerite apparently lived a happy life together until he died from pneumonia in Vancouver in June 1922 at the age of 62.

He had invested in Seattle real estate and built an apartment house and hotel, which brought him an income of $500 a month, and operated a mine in California. He left a healthy estate, which his wife, who died in California in 1949, inherited.

Charley and Jim honored by Dominion of Canada

Tagish Charley and Skookum Jim were made honorary citizens of the Dominion of Canada for their part in discovering the Klondike gold. Charley sold his mining properties in 1901. He spent the rest of his life at Carcross where he bought the Carcross Hotel, entertained lavishly, gambled frequently, and finally, on Dec. 26, 1908, during a drunken spree, fell off a bridge and drowned at the age of 42.

Skookum Jim lived in Carcross during the fall and winter. He returned to the Klondike each year for spring cleanup. He spent quite a bit of time in the Dawson jail, too, for being drunk and disorderly.

Jim finally sold his Klondike mines to the Lewis River Mining and Dredging Company for $65,000 in 1904, and then spent the next

Skookum Jim and Kate moved back to Carcross, originally named Caribou Crossing.

10 years traveling ceaselessly across the North vainly seeking another gold claim – even though his mining property paid him royalties of $90,000 a year. So fierce was his quest, that in the end, his magnificent physique was weakened and he died, worn out, on July 11, 1916.

Henderson outlived them all. He was belatedly recognized as a co-discoverer of the Klondike and was given a pension of $200 a month. For the rest of his life, he continued to look for gold and died in 1933, talking of the big strike he still hoped to find.

Klondike nuggets given to U.S. President

Carmack had saved 22 nuggets from the first pans of dirt he worked out at Bonanza Creek. In 1909 these nuggets were made into a telegraph key that was presented to President Taft and used by him in opening the Alaska-Yukon Exposition in Seattle.

The exposition was not the only thing opened up by Klondike gold. In 1896, the United States was in the third year of a severe depression. Banks failed right and left, and there was unemployment from coast to coast. Heavy exports of gold had depleted the country's treasury. The Klondike gold loosened up capital all over the world, stimulated inventiveness and gave employment to many. It helped

A telegraph key made of 22 gold nuggets was given to President Taft in 1909 at the Alaska-Yukon Exposition in Seattle. This photo shows Expo buildings on the University of Washington campus.

San Francisco, revived Portland, Ore., and was the making of Seattle. It was the last of the great international gold rushes.

"There has been nothing like the Klondike before, there has been nothing like it since, and there can never be anything like it again," wrote Pierre Berton in his book, "Klondike Fever."

Carmack's Rabbit Creek discovery, later known as Bonanza, drew many prospectors with Klondike fever north to dig their fortunes from the gold-laden land. Most did not succeed in realizing their dreams, but one man who was in the bar at Fortymile when Carmack first told of his find became rich beyond his wildest expectations.

18

LUCKIEST MAN ON THE KLONDIKE

A few years before Lady Luck showered riches on Clarence Berry, the "luckiest man on the Klondike" didn't have enough money to pay his room rent. Caught in the panic of 1893, he was flat broke. He couldn't even ask his sweetheart, Ethel Bush, to marry him and saw no particular prospect of ever being able to do so.

In the Fresno Valley of California where he raised fruit, Berry appeared destined to a life of hard, plodding work for a bare living. So when he heard about riches coming out of the earth in the North, he jumped at the chance to try for the "gold ring."

That he succeeded in his quest, and held on to his wealth, was attested to by the Gold Room built at the University of Alaska Museum in Fairbanks. Built with money provided through a special grant from the Berry Holding Company of Fresno, Calif., it was a "belated gesture by family members in recognition of the part that the frozen frontier and mining industry has played in our fortunes," according to company spokesperson C.J. Bennett.

The benefactors of the museum wanted to display rocker boxes, gold scales and other early day mining equipment, as well as gold like the $130,000 worth of nuggets Berry brought "Outside" when the historic gold ships *Portland* and *Excelsior* landed at Seattle and San Francisco with news of the gold strikes. That news electrified the nation and started the gold rush of 1898.

Not many other original prospectors who located gold on Eldorado and Bonanza creeks held on to their riches. Berry not only held on, but added to his wealth. The "sober, honest, hard-working, ambitious, home-loving Californian," as folks described him, wasn't spoiled by his good luck. And Mrs. Eli Gage said he was the "most modest millionaire I ever saw."

Berry borrowed money to head north

But before good fortune changed his life, the young man had to scrape up the money for his trip north in 1894. He borrowed his capital, which has been estimated between $40 and $60, at an exorbitant rate of interest, and it took all but $5 to reach Juneau.

During the early 1890s, Juneau was alive with men on their way to the goldfields. Berry, a giant of a man with the biceps of a blacksmith, joined a party of 40 attempting to make it over Chilkoot Pass. His two big arms, sturdy legs and courage to spare brought him through, although 37 of the original party turned back when storms destroyed their outfits. Borrowing bacon and other supplies to get through, Berry and two others pushed on, arriving at Fortymile with little more than the clothes on their backs.

Clarence Berry joined a party of 40 men climbing the Chilkoot Pass trail in 1894 – all but three of them turned back after storms destroyed their provisions.

Berry didn't find riches at first, but he did find work at $100 a month, and soon he secured a claim. His prospects looked bright enough that the following year he returned to California to marry Ethel.

It took Clarence and his new bride, Ethel, three months to travel from Juneau to Fortymile by dog sled, a distance of about 900 miles.

The "Bride of the Klondike's" novel experience of going over the Divide, and her life in a mining camp in the frozen North, made her advice to other women travelers valuable.

New bride gives advice

In an interview reported by John W. Leonard in "Gold Fields of the Klondike," published in 1897, Ethel Berry is quoted as saying:

"What advice would I give to a woman about going to Alaska? Why, to stay away, of course. It's no place for a woman. I mean for a woman alone; one who goes to make a living or a fortune. It's much better for a man, though, if he has a wife along – after a man has worked hard all day in the diggings, he doesn't feel much like cooking a nice meal when he goes to his cabin, cold, tired and hungry, to find no fire in the stove and all the food frozen."

She convinced Berry she could be helpful to him – worth more in his venture than any man. Moreover, the trip would be certainly novel; not at all like the usual honeymoon trip to Niagara Falls. Her arguments must have been persuasive, for Berry agreed to bring her back with him.

And her honeymoon was different, all right. Strapped to a sled, the bride made the trip over the mountains pulled by her new husband. Her trousseau, especially made for the trip, cost $250 and consisted of heavy woolen underwear, knitted woolen stockings, flannels and furs.

Three-month trek to the Klondike

It took the young couple three months to travel from Juneau to Fortymile, a distance of about 900 miles. They made 10 to 12 miles, occasionally 15, a day by dog team, which they'd picked up at Dyea.

"We couldn't do more, because the dogs couldn't stand it," Ethel later said.

Berry built a log house for his new wife, with holes for doors and windows and no floor. Ethel had a little sheet iron stove to cook on that had holes on top, and for baking she used a metal drum. The newlyweds endured hardships without complaining, for they had high hopes of the pot of gold at the end of the rainbow.

The Berrys lived in a log cabin that Clarence Berry built on their gold claim.

Their hopes looked dim at first, for the claims at Fortymile yielded no gold. To make ends meet, Berry took a job tending bar at Bill McPhee's saloon.

He was bartending the day that George Washington Carmack came rushing in to tell of striking it rich on the Throndiuk – the Indian word for Klondike – and McPhee earned Berry's undying gratitude by grubstaking him for the stampede.

While bartending at Fortymile, Clarence Berry heard firsthand from George W. Carmack about the riches in Bonanza Creek.

"Sure, Clarence," McPhee said, according to Judge James Wickersham in his book, "Old Yukon." "Here's the key to the cache. Help yourself."

Berry never forgot McPhee's generosity, and he later repaid the saloon owner many times over.

Berry stakes claim

The well-provisioned Berry led stampeders from the Alaska side of the line over the upriver trail to Carmack's Klondike. There, Berry staked "Forty Above" on Bonanza. He didn't believe in putting all his eggs in one basket, however, and when the opportunity came to exchange a half interest in his Bonanza claim for half of Anton Stander's claim No. 6 on Eldorado Creek, he lost no time in making the trade. In addition, he and his partner bought No. 4 and 5 on Eldorado.

He and Stander left Fortymile for the winter's mining. Night after night they burned the frozen ground; day after day, they shoveled up what they had thawed. Heartening news came from Bonanza on "Twenty-one Above" in October. Louis Rhodes had reached bedrock, apparently the first to do so in the Klondike. At the bottom of his shaft he found gravel studded with glittering gold.

In early November, Berry and Stander reached bedrock, too, and soon realized they were working the richest ground either had ever seen or heard about. They began hiring men to work for them, and a daily payroll of $150 was taken care of by panning for only a few minutes in the evening of a tiny portion of the day's diggings. By Christmas, Clarence and Ethel were showing visitors three preserve jars, each of which held gold washed from a single pan (two shovels full) of bedrock gravel.

Gold abounds in Klondike

Three brothers named Scouse on "Fifteen" made an even more spectacular strike – "nuggets stuck out of the gravel like raisins in a pudding." These three claims proved that the Klondike was one of the world's richest mining districts.

Miners had to thaw the ground, take out loads of dirt, and then thaw the next layer to get down to bedrock.

The Berry brothers, who later joined the group, cleaned up on No. 4 Eldorado.

"Not in total quality," wrote Pierre Berton in his book, "Klondike Fever," "but most certainly wealthy in some of the individual claims."

A fraction too long

Berry and Stander had bought adjacent claims from the original stakers and were mining the upper end of "Claim Five" when government surveyor Maj. William Ogilvie discovered the claim was too long by a fraction totaling 41 feet, six inches. He made the discovery on a bitterly cold spring day, about 10 degrees below zero, and recalls the experience in his book, "Early Days in the Yukon:"

"I reached the claim just as the men were quitting work in the shaft below ... I turned to my notes to figure out the length of the claim. I never suspected a fraction here – and such a fraction! Possibly in all the history of gold mining, none was ever found richer; single pans – two shovels of dirt – were found in it with values as high as $150 in gold."

When the *S.S. Excelsior* docked in San Francisco on July 14, 1897, the Berrys told reporters, "The Klondike is the richest gold field in the world." Clarence and Ethel then carried sacks, jars and bottles filled with gold off the steamship.

Berry almost loses claim

Nearly all the work done so far had been done on this fraction, Ogilvie noted, and he knew what a wild scramble, perhaps even mayhem, would ensue if the knowledge leaked out that the fraction existed. Berry would lose everything he had worked for that winter, too.

Although Ogilvie was a very conscientious, honest official, he made up his mind to keep quiet about the fraction. He assisted Berry to have a friend stake it and then transfer the fraction to Berry. In return, Berry's friend, George Byrne, got an equal length off the lower end of the property, so Berry's block would remain unbroken.

DREAMS OF GOLD

"A friend like that, in such a need, is a friend, indeed," Ogilvie wrote.

Gold was everywhere on the Berry's claim. When Ethel needed pocket money, she just walked to the dump, and with a sharp stick, she smashed the frozen clumps of dirt apart to find nuggets. She picked nuggets on her walks as aimlessly as other women picked flowers. When it came time to go "Outside," she had collected $10,000 worth.

When spring came, two little steamers chugged down the Yukon River – the *Alice* and the *Portus B. Weare*. Their decks were crowded with Eldorado and Bonanza kings, hailing from every part of the globe. On board, too, were Clarence and Ethel Berry, knowing that they were worth at least $1 million. When they reached St. Michael, they found two ocean-going vessels, the N.A.T. Company's *Portland* and the A.C. Company's *Excelsior*.

Word of gold spreads Outside

As the Berry's boarded the *Excelsior* bound for San Francisco, friends helped them drag a sagging suitcase and two wooden boxes filled with gold aboard. The couple laughed and chattered like excited children. Clarence promised his wife the diamond wedding ring he at last could afford, and they talked of the farm they would buy – the farm where Berry had once worked for starvation wages.

Although the *Portland* had sailed first, the *Excelsior* won the race and had already landed in San Francisco on July 14 when the *Portland* pulled into Seattle on July 17, 1897. The news of the gold strike and the word "Klondike" soon was on everyone's lips.

At 9 a.m. a special issue of The Seattle Post-Intelligencer hit the streets with the whole front page devoted to the story of the Portland and her golden load.

"At 3 o'clock this morning, the steamship *Portland*, from St. Michael for Seattle, passed up the Sound with more than a ton of solid gold on board and 68 passengers. In the captain's office are three chests and a large safe filled with precious nuggets. The metal is worth nearly $700,000 and most of it was taken out of the ground in less than three months last winter. In size the nuggets range from the size of a pea to a guinea egg. Of the 68 miners aboard, hardly a man has less than $7,000 and one or two have more than $100,000 in yellow nuggets."

"Show us the gold," the crowd, 5,000 strong, shouted as they crammed onto Schwabacher's Dock one hour after the *Portland* had tied up. The miners onboard the *Portland* lifted their sacks of gold dust and nuggets in response.

"The Klondike is the richest gold field in the world," Berry told reporters who besieged him in his hotel room. Four sacks of nuggets on the floor, and jars and bottles on the table, all filled with gold, bore witness to his words. He and Ethel were so beleaguered, and followed everywhere they went, that they finally fled to rural California.

Berrys return to mine for more

In the summer of 1898, Clarence and Ethel traveled back over the Chilkoot Pass, taking other family members to help work their claims. They enjoyed a peculiar luxury this time. The only cow in the area, munching $400-a-ton hay, supplied the ex-fruit farmer from Fresno with fresh milk. Berry, always hospitable, had in front of his cabin a container full of gold and a bottle of whiskey with the invitation, "Help yourself."

The Berrys received $2 million for their claims and the Monte Carlo saloon when they moved on from the Klondike. Berry's luck stayed with him, though, for he struck it rich again on Ester Creek in the Fairbanks region. Most of the Berry claims there were filed in 1903 and patented in 1911. One hundred miles east of Fairbanks on the Steese Highway lies what is left of the Berry Camp on Mastodon Fork and Eagle Creek. Mining along Mastodon brought in gold royalties as late as 1957.

Berrys invest in oil

When the Berry brothers left Alaska, they put their new-found wealth from northern gold fields into California oil fields, founding the Berry Holding Company and various other enterprises. They made another fortune. The companies are still in business, producing from the original properties discovered and developed by Clarence and Henry Berry and carried on by other family members. Clarence died in 1930; his brother, Henry, at one time owner of the Los Angeles Angels, died in 1929.

Clarence Berry never forgot his original grubstaker, Bill McPhee. In 1906, fire destroyed McPhee's saloon, and well along in years, McPhee lost everything but the clothes he was wearing. From San Francisco, Berry wired that McPhee should draw on him for all he needed to get back in business. Later, in McPhee's declining years, he lived on a pension provided by the grateful Berry.

A bronze plaque commemorating Clarence Berry's role and contribution to the mining industry in the Yukon and Alaska was put on display in the Gold Room at the University of Alaska Fairbanks. Annual scholarships still are awarded for the mining school for promising and deserving students as a living memorial to the "luckiest man in the Klondike."

The rich discoveries made by Berry and Carmack also helped to increase the fortunes of the man who turned a patch of barren land into one of the most famous gold-rush towns ever known.

After the Berrys left the Klondike, they switched from mining gold nuggets to finding black gold in the oil-rich land of northern California.

RUSH TO THE KLONDIKE

19

DAWSON IS BORN

When an enterprising businessman along the Sixty-mile River heard about the rich ore found by George Washington Carmack and Clarence Berry on Rabbit Creek in 1896, he loaded a raft with lumber from his sawmill and drifted down to the mouth of the Klondike River. On Aug. 28, Joseph Ladue staked the boggy flats to the northeast of the mouth as a town

Tents line the riverbank in 1896 on land that soon would become Dawson City.

site and named it after George M. Dawson, head of the Geological Survey of Canada who had surveyed the area and noted its possibilities for gold a decade before.

Ladue had a knack for being in the right place at the right time. Born in Schuyler Falls, N.Y., in 1855, he arrived in the boomtown of Deadwood, Ariz., at the age of 21 with $100 in his pocket. He got a job working as a general laborer, but soon got hired as an engineer at a mine for $4 per day, despite never having operated a steam engine before.

Within 18 months, he was the night-shift foreman at the Hidden Treasure gold mine and soon thereafter landed a $10-a-day job as a superintendent overseeing a 60-stamp mill.

Ladue drawn north

His adventurous nature drew him north in 1881, and after a short stint at the Treadwell Mine in Juneau, he crossed the Chilkoot Pass into the Yukon, along with 50 other men who crossed over the Chilkoot Pass that year. He tested creeks and spent the following winter at Fort Reliance.

Ladue joined up with Jack McQuestern and Arthur Harper to trade along the river, and during his travels, he met the exploration

A group of men pose in front of the Dawson Town Site Company and Harper & Ladue Mill Company office in Dawson City around 1896.

party of U.S. Army Lt. Frederick Schwatka near the Alaska-Yukon border. Ladue didn't think Schwatka's raft would make the journey all the way down the Yukon, and he tried to sell the lieutenant a small scow.

When Schwatka turned down the offer, Ladue hopped on the explorer's raft and floated with the party another 350 miles down to Fort Yukon.

The miner-turned-trader and his business partners established a new post at the mouth of Sixtymile River in 1893 and named it Ogilvie, in honor of Maj. William Ogilvie, the first government official they had met. Ladue set up his sawmill next to the post after trading slowed down, and supplied the miners with the lumber they needed to build sluice boxes and other necessities.

Ladue predicts gold-filled district

Ladue knew in his heart that the district had mining potential and grubstaked Robert Henderson, the man who had offended George

Steamboats like the *Chas. H. Hamilton* and *Columbian* discharged passengers and cargo at the new town of Dawson during the Klondike Gold Rush.

Washington Carmack by speaking ill of his Native friends. When Henderson returned to Ogilvie and told Ladue of his discovery, Ladue was ecstatic and knew his prediction about the area had come true.

By Oct. 1, 1896, Ladue had moved his sawmill to Dawson and the settlement started to grow. He sold the first lots for between $5 and $25. There were two log cabins, a small warehouse, the sawmill and a few tents, with a total population of 25 men and one woman. Ladue sold all the rough lumber his small mill could produce at $140 per thousand feet to the miners working on Rabbit Creek, which had been renamed Bonanza.

As word of the rich discoveries spread, more and more people headed north. Before the ice had cleared from the river, the largest rush yet to be seen in the north was under way. By late July 1897, the district had 5,000 people and Ladue raised his lot prices to between $800 and $8,000. Town lots later fetched $40,000.

The rush is on

The arrival of the gold-laden steamships *Excelsior* and *Portland* into U.S. ports during the summer of 1897 triggered a continent-wide rush that culminated in the stampede of 1898.

On July 14, the day the passengers from the *Excelsior* unloaded their $500,000 in gold in San Francisco, an ad from The Seattle Daily Times stated:

"Now is the time to go to the rich Klondyke country, where according to last reports, gold is as plentiful as sawdust."

Within three days of that ad, the *Portland* pulled up to Seattle's Schwabacher Dock and unloaded 68 passengers, 40 of whom were miners, and about $1 million in gold.

It's estimated that 100,000 set out on the rugged journey north, and that between 30,000 and 50,000 actually reached the Klondike area. Dawson became the largest city north of San Francisco and west of Winnipeg and boasted nearly 40,000 residents at its height, providing those citizens with steam heating, running water, electricity and phone service.

In no time at all, Dawson resembled a large cosmopolitan city with dozens of hotels, motion picture theaters, a hospital and many restaurants. But despite its amenities, Dawson lacked sewer and garbage disposal systems. By midsummer, the entire city was a reeking swamp. Malaria and typhoid epidemics swept over the city, and scurvy also was prevalent due to poor diets.

Newspapers tell of gold strikes

The newspapers of the day kept the populace apprised of social events, crime and new gold discoveries, which often ended in stampedes of hopeful miners yet to make their fortunes. The following article in the June 17, 1899, issue of The Klondike Nugget is typical of such notices:

"Another stampede out of Dawson, and one which possesses

On July 17, 1897, when the steamship *Portland* arrived in Seattle with 68 passengers and around $1 million in gold onboard, the crowd of 5,000 on Schwabacher's Dock shouted, "Show us the gold!" Over the next few years, close to 100,000 people stampeded to the North Country hoping to strike it rich.

After word of the gold discoveries on the Klondike hit "Outside," thousands of hopeful prospectors headed to the gold fields via the Chilkoot Pass trail.

more than the usual amount of merit, took place this week as a result of the arrival in the city of Pat E. Dunden, Messrs. Pearl, Crane and others from the waters of the upper White River. They reported the discovery of gold on what has been named California Creek, a tributary of the White River, and showed several samples of the precious metal, which they found at a depth of fifteen feet. Several of the discoverers recorded immediately, and Gold Commissioner Senkler posted a notice of the discovery at his office.

"Three members of the party came down the White and Yukon rivers on a raft, while the others walked in, striking the city via Swede Creek, which, they say, is the proper trail to take. The new creek heads in the vicinity of Glacier and Miller creeks of the Fortymile district, both of which have been gold producers. The reason it had not been heard of earlier is because the prospectors had been making their headquarters principally at Fortymile. Among the Dawsonites who went on the stampede is Policy Bob, who claims to have had men at work on the creek all winter."

Dancehall girls mine the miners

While many miners worked long hours trying to find gold along the creeks in the Klondike, Dawson's dancehall girls offered a welcome diversion from the grueling, lonely days of digging in the subarctic tundra.

"The sourdoughs lay on their bunks until noon — and noon might just as well be any other time — moving painfully about only to stoke the stove or break off a chunk of rye bread, more from sheer boredom than hunger," wrote Ellis Lucia about digging for gold during a winter in the North Country in "Klondike Kate: The Life of the Queen of the Klondike."

Hard-working miners looked to saloons and dancehalls, like the Savoy Bar in Dawson, as an escape from their back-breaking and often lonely work in the gold fields.

Front Street in Dawson was a booming place by 1899.

"Many were ill with dysentery and scurvy, and worst of all, the sickening depression of futility. At times the men entered into the awful bleakness to claw at the frozen ground of their claims. They returned to the drafty warmth of their cabins, holding stiffened fingers above the stove, to ask themselves aloud just why they were trapped here in this Godforsaken wilderness. ...

"Half-crazed with cabin fever, the sourdoughs could stand it no longer. Climbing into bulky mackinaws, mukluks and fur caps, they stuffed fat buckskin pokes into their coats and headed for Dawson City ... It was a gay, frolicsome world, filled with fun in contrast with the awful silence of the outer wilderness ... Thousands in yellow gold changed hands in the gambling halls, to be lost and won again, and then to be lost once more to a pretty bit of fluff who called you honey, gave you a nice smile and a peck on the cheek, and would be your very own for the evening if you kept the champagne flowing her way. But you didn't mind, for there was plenty more of this yellow stuff where that came from. ..."

Gold changes hands

The technique used by most dancehall girls to separate the gold miners from their wealth included getting the prospectors drunk in private boxes that surrounded dance floors in saloons. In her book "Good Time Girls," Lael Morgan shares a detailed account of the separation process as told by La Belle Brooks-Vincent:

"She is all nerve as she enters a room and surveys the waiting crowd ... The dancehall girl is industrious. She is never vacillating or undecided; she is persevering. She does not flit about the room bestowing a smile here, a caress there and again a pouting neglect. When she selects her victim she stays with him. The more marked her favor, the greater his triumph ... He needs her to complete a spectacle of himself as a favored beau. ..."

Most of the "victims" were willing single men who prospected alone and didn't have women waiting for them back home. And they enjoyed the company of the dancehall girls, many of whom eventually ended up as wealthy as some of the miners themselves.

"The poor ginks just gotta spend it," said Diamond Tooth Gertie Lovejoy, one of Dawson's most famous dancehall girls. "They're scared they'll die before they get it out of the ground."

Folks lodged few criminal complaints against the dancehall girls, show girls or prostitutes during the early days of the gold rush in Dawson.

"Women of any sort were such a rare commodity that even prostitutes were tolerated and given a degree of protection by the North West Mounted Police," wrote Frances Backhouse, author of "Women of the Klondike."

But by 1900, when Dawson had real-city advantages like electricity, telegraph service, a post office and schools, families began migrating into town and some citizens started to campaign for eliminating the red-light district.

A few prostitutes peek out of their "cribs" in Lousetown in 1899.

Many prostitutes moved their operations across the river to Klondike City in 1901. Also known as Lousetown and White Chapel, it remained a hub of activity well beyond the height of the gold rush.

In her book, "Good Time Girls," Lael Morgan quotes schoolteacher Laura Beatrice Berton, who spied on the district one afternoon in 1908.

"At the back doors of the tiny frame houses, the whores, laughing and singing, calling out to each other and chattering like bright birds, were making their toilets for the evening. Some were washing their long hair – invariably bright gold or jet black – drying it in the sun and leisurely brushing it out. Others were just reclining languorously and gossiping with their neighbors. Some were singing lyrically. All were in their chemises. ..."

Queen of the Yukon susceptible to fire

But along with the gaiety, Dawson also had its share of tragedy. Fire was the curse of many towns during the gold-rush era, and Dawson was no exception. The extreme cold, coupled with dryness, meant fires burned in all buildings when occupied.

Stove pipes thrust through flimsy walls or roofs of cabins and tents carried smoke from high-creosote spruce. Over time, the creosote built up on the pipes, which increased the draft and eventually created enough heat to start the creosote burning. A red-hot stove pipe could set a building on fire.

The Dawson volunteer fire department built a fire hall and tower down near the bank of the Yukon River by 1897. Whenever a report of

As happened many times during the early gold-rush days, Dawson buildings caught fire on Oct. 14, 1898, and again on April 26, 1899, destroying more than 100 buildings.

The Dawson Fire Department stood at the ready to help hose down fires in its gold-rush town.

a fire came, firemen rang the bell in the tower and raced to the scene, pulling their firefighting apparatus behind them. Twenty-two alarms in one night was the record.

The fire department had a hose cart, which extended only as far as the city's water system, and chemical carts that were little more than large fire extinguishers to use when water froze inside the hoses. By the time an alarm sounded and the firemen reached a fire, they usually found the tent or cabin gone and spent most of their time trying to keep the fire away from other structures.

Blankets used to keep fires at bay

To keep fires from spreading during cold weather, residents had a rather unique system. They soaked blankets in water, thrust them out windows and fastened them over walls. The blankets promptly froze and formed a barrier of ice.

But as the town grew by leaps and bounds, the residents needed better fire protection in order to get fire insurance. Insurance companies wouldn't cover high-risk areas, at least not at rates that most customers could pay.

Some sources say that town merchants collected $5 apiece from the ladies of the evening to buy a fire engine. Others speculate that the ladies collected the money from the merchants and politicians who used their services.

New steam pumper proves useless

Whatever the real story, the town purchased a steam-pumper from the Seattle Fire Department in 1898 and had it shipped north. However, due to human error, the new horse-drawn fire engine with its smoking stack proved useless when a fire broke out on April 26, 1899. The next day, the Klondike Nugget reported on the disaster.

"Dawson is once again in ashes. The Queen of the Yukon is once more attacked by her old-time enemy. The city's loss will be fully a

The citizens of Dawson relied on the fire department and its hose wagon, steam pumper and other equipment to put out the regularly occurring fires that started because everyone used wood stoves for heat.

million dollars. One hundred and eleven buildings gone up in smoke and flame. Incompetency in operating the Fire Steamer charged with being the cause of the heavy loss.

"The fire found its origin in the apartment of Helen Holden, located in the second floor of the Bodega Saloon on the west side of First Avenue. Of this there is not the least doubt, reports to the contrary notwithstanding. The first jet of smoke curled from the building at about half-past seven o'clock.

"It was seen almost immediately by Fireman Farrell who came with lightning step to the fire station and turned in an alarm. The response was prompt enough to win the favor of all who saw the rush of the gallant fire boys and hope was seen in every face. No time was lost in hurrying the steamer to its position on the river and then came the anxious wait for the water."

No water to put out the flames

"Five minutes went slowly by, then ten minutes more slowly still, and yet no water filled the waiting lines of hose or gladdened the hearts of the gallant fellows who waited, nozzle in hand, for the saving fluid," the newspaper article said.

"It was 25 minutes before the water flowed on its way to the fire and it was during that dreadful period that the thin curl of smoke, which Farrell had seen, grew into a huge volume and the little blaze beneath expanded until it had become a roaring, all-powerful body. When the water came, it was too late to stay the fire in the course of the wind, and its march of devastation depended only upon the quantity of material lying in its path."

While many people said the fire was "an act of God," several others said it was aided by the stupidity of man. It seems, that during breakup, the river had churned under the rotting ice and the shift in pressure had pushed water up through the hole where the steamer sat. Nobody noticed that the water had doused the fire in the fire box, which was necessary to make the steam-pumper work.

It took almost a half-hour to get the fire lit again, by which time the entire east side of Dawson had already gone up in flames.

Ladue wasn't around to see his city go up in smoke. He'd left in 1897 to return to New York, where he married his childhood sweetheart, Anna "Kitty" Mason. But the years of privation in the Far North had taken their toll, and he died from tuberculosis on June 27, 1900, less than three years after realizing his dream of riches.

The Flame of the Yukon

Dawson always managed to rebuild itself after devastating fires, however, and again had become a center of entertainment when a flame of another sort arrived in 1900. Following brief stints in Skagway and Whitehorse, Kansas-born Kathleen Eloisa Rockwell swirled her way into gold-rush history when she stepped on stage at the Palace Grand.

Kathleen Eloisa Rockwell, also known as Klondike Kate, whirled her way across dance-hall stages in the Yukon, delighting her audiences with her moves and fancy costumes.

Better known as "Klondike Kate," she delighted audiences of miners with her song-and-dance routines. She wore an enormous cape and an elaborate dress covered in red sequins in one dance that made her famous. Kate would take the cape off and start leaping and twirling with a cane that had 200 yards of red chiffon attached. Onlookers said she looked like fire dancing around.

At the end of her number, Kate dramatically dropped to the floor. The miners, who went wild for the redheaded beauty, named her "The Flame of the Yukon."

Kate reportedly made $200 a week for her number and

an additional $500 a night after her performances for being "a good listener" to lonely miners. She claimed to have spent much of her fortune on fine clothes and jewelry – boasting later in life that she wore "$1,500 gowns from Paris and bracelets of the purest gold."

But even though Kate had a successful stage life for a couple of years, her love life proved less fruitful. She fell for Alexander Pantages, owner of Dawson's Orpheum Theatre on Front Street, and he convinced her to invest in a string of theaters in the Pacific Northwest and start their own theater company.

Kate's love life goes bust

Kate invested with Pantages, but when he asked her to head south, she hesitated. She began to drink and party heavily, according to Morgan, who wrote that Pantages loved Kate and tried to keep their relationship going, but Kate loved liquor and the thrill of the gold rush more than her lover.

In later years, Kate claimed that Pantages left her, but it appears that wasn't the case.

He kept trying to get her to quit drinking and to join him, but finally gave up and married Lois Mendenhall, a violin-playing vaudeville performer, in 1905.

Kate, shocked at the marriage, filed a lawsuit for $25,000 against Pantages for breach of promise to marry her. Morgan wrote that Kate claimed Pantages had "injured, damaged, humiliated, and disgraced her, causing her to suffer anguish of mind."

The case was settled quickly out of court, and the settlement has been reported from $5,000 on up to $60,000.

Although Kate, who later settled in Oregon, led neither an exciting nor a very lucrative life once she left Dawson, she spent some time in Fairbanks and then went on the circuit doing song-and-dance routines in the States.

In 1931, a Norwegian named Johnny Matson entered her life. Matson, who'd mined in the Klondike and had been smitten with Kate for 30 years, finally got around to telling her how he felt.

He wrote her about their meeting back at the turn of the century.

That letter began two years of correspondence, which finally led to marriage in 1933 when Matson was around 70 and Kate was 57. Matson died in 1946.

Two years later, Kate married William L. Van Duren, age 71.

Kate actively promoted herself and the gold-rush legends, which she helped to create, well into her 60s. She excelled at self-promotion, traveling the lecture circuit around the Lower 48 expounding on her legend and capitalizing on her life as "Queen of the Yukon," "Belle of Dawson" and "Klondike Queen," as she called herself.

If she wasn't dressing up for a holiday parade, reports say "she might be seen rolling her own cigarette with the deftness of a cowboy."

She later became a recluse and died on Feb. 21, 1957, at the age of 80.

Another Kate surfaces in the Klondike

Ill-fated love led a Canadian girl to set out for the Klondike in 1898. When Katherine Ryan heard Vancouver, B.C., newspaper boys screaming headlines about gold found in the Yukon, she decided to head off into the rugged terrain and seek an adventure.

Katherine Ryan, a nurse, trudged to the Klondike in 1898.

Ryan was the authentic Kate, according to Ann Brennan in her book, "The Real Klondike Kate." She'd first made her way to Seattle, then Vancouver, after she'd given her heart to a man who would never be hers. She'd fallen in love with Simon Gallagher, part of the local gentry from her hometown of Johnville, a rural community northeast of Bath in Carleton County.

Gallagher's mother, however, would not allow the two of them to be together, since Ryan was from a poor family and not worthy of her son. After the mother insisted her son enter the seminary, Ryan headed to Seattle to become a nurse in 1893.

When she heard the news of gold strikes in the Klondike, the 28-year-old hopped onboard a steamship bound for Southeast Alaska in February 1898. While thousands of stampeders headed to the Klondike via the Chilkoot Trail out of Skagway, Kate Ryan chose the less traveled Stikine River route out of Wrangell.

In Wrangell, she offered to cook for a group of North West Mounted Police, who then gratefully included her with their group to hike the muddy and brutal Stikine trail. They trudged through deep snow, praying the weather would not warm and turn the river into a torrent of wet fury.

When the policemen stopped to make a permanent camp, Kate continued on alone in her quest to reach Glenora, a tiny settlement built for about a dozen people that had swelled to more than 3,000 as prospectors streamed in on their way to the Klondike.

In 1897, Fort Wrangell consisted of only a few buildings along the water's edge.

Kate Ryan spent a summer in Glenora, pictured here at the turn-of-the-last century, where she operated a restaurant in a new hotel and washed clothes to earn money.

Kate spent the summer in Glenora, operating a restaurant in a new hotel and washing clothes. Then she bought supplies and continued her journey, leading a string of pack horses up the trail from Glenora to Telegraph Creek and on to the Teslin Trail.

She swapped her horses for a sled and dog team in Teslin City, and made her way to Atlin camp, 60 miles away, where she'd heard her medical skills were needed.

Atlin, which consisted of a few log buildings and half-a-dozen tents in winter 1898, proved to be a challenge for Kate. She started another restaurant in a 12-foot-by-14-foot canvas tent and practiced her nursing upon the sick.

The next spring, she packed up her meager belongings and walked on to Whitehorse. There she pitched her tent, put on a pot of coffee and hung a sign reading "Kate's Café" outside the door. After two years, she built one of the first frame houses in Whitehorse and took space in a new hotel for her restaurant.

Whitehorse served as a storage point for Yukon River boats during the winter.

When the Mounties approached her and asked if she'd consider becoming the first "constable special" to guard women in the Whitehorse jail, she agreed. With a height approaching six feet, she never had any problems with the "troubled" women she came across.

Except one.

Kate Ryan, who had become affectionately known as "Klondike Kate" by those who knew of her fortitude, kindness and immense accomplishments, didn't like people thinking she was the famous stage dancer Kate Rockwell.

Kathleen Eloisa "Kitty" Rockwell already had a colorful past when she arrived in Whitehorse. She was a singer, a dancer, a prostitute and a thief, according to Brennan. And she earned

Kate Ryan was affectionately called "Klondike Kate" by those close to her, and she didn't like being confused with the notorious dancehall girl.

a 30-day sentence of hard labor in Ryan's jail for practicing her shady shenanigans.

When she moved on to Dawson and started calling herself "Klondike Kate," rumors of all sorts traveled back to Kate Ryan's hometown.

Kate Ryan tried her best to assure her devoutly Catholic community, family and friends that she was not the notorious dancer.

Ryan, who never married, remained in Whitehorse until 1919 raising her widowed brother's sons, running her business and working as a gold inspector for the Mounted Police. She died peacefully in Vancouver in 1932.

20

St. Michael awakens

Dawson wasn't the only town to spring up as a result of the Klondike discoveries. A Russian village at the mouth of the Yukon River also turned into a hustling, bustling frontier town as thousands of prospectors flooded into the region.

The arrival of the gold-laden steamer *Alice* into St. Michael in June 1897 signaled the beginning of the Klondike Gold Rush.

On June 25, 1897, the sleepy old Russian town of St. Michael awoke when the river steamer *Alice* arrived with 25 miners from Dawson carrying $500,000 among them in gold dust. That was enough to liven up just about any town.

But the party wasn't over. Two days later, the *Portus B. Weare* carried in another group of successful men who staggered off the small steamer with pokes of gold estimated to be worth up to $175,000.

News of the large gold strike in the Klondike hit newspapers across America after the steamship *Portland* docked in Seattle with 68 miners and more than $1 million in gold aboard.

And more miners followed. St. Michael became the hub for those with visions of nuggets dancing before their eyes, both coming from and going to the rich fields in the Yukon.

Along with dynamic headlines coming from The Seattle Post-Intellingencer, glowing reports like the following excerpt from the Aug. 8, 1897, edition of the New York World newspaper helped fuel the stampede for gold.

"Mr. J. O. Hestwod, one of the most successful Argonauts of '97, has just returned from Klondike and furnishes by telegraph to the Sunday World a true picture of Alaska as it really is. He said:

'Modern or ancient history records nothing so rich in extent as the recent discoveries of gold on the tributaries of the Yukon River.

'The few millions of dollars recently turned into the banks and smelters of Seattle and San Francisco from the Klondike district is but a slight indication of what is to follow in the near future. When we consider the fact that there is scarcely a shovelful of soil in Alaska and the Northwest Territory that does not yield grains of gold in appreciable quantities, who can compute the value of the golden treasure that this great country will yield in the next few years?

'The Yukon River, which forms a great artery flowing through this frozen, rock-ribbed region for 2,600 miles, seems to be a providential highway, opened up for the pioneer gold hunters and their followers, who are numbered by thousands yearly. There is room in that country for 100,000 miners for 100 years. I do not make this statement from what someone else has told me, or from what I have read. I speak from actual experience in that land of gold.' "

Soon after the *Portland* arrived, hopeful people from all walks of life abandoned their duties and left for the Klondike. Boats of all kinds, including the *Australia* pictured above in 1897, sailed north from Seattle, nearly bursting with people, gear and pack animals. During the next few years, thousands of Klondikers made the trek toward Canada and Alaska, but few found the fortunes that drew them north.

For those with money, steamers chugging the all-water route from Seattle to St. Michael afforded a less arduous route at the onset for prospectors to get to the gold-rich fields near Dawson. Passengers aboard steamships headed north also could enjoy a drink in relative comfort.

Glowing reports lure stampeders

Such glowing reports convinced thousands that they should leave life as they knew it and travel to the gold-rich fields of the Klondike.

Many of the stampeders decided to travel by an all-water route. They took large steamships from Seattle to St. Michael, but then had to find alternative means to travel the Yukon River to Dawson.

The Yukon River carries about two-thirds the volume of water of the mighty Mississippi and is loaded in the summer with soil debris of ground glacial rock and silt from banks cut by the current.

The debris, deposited on the wide, fan-shaped flats that reached out into the Bering Sea, prohibited large ocean ships from entering into the deep current of the stream. All passengers and cargo had to land at St. Michael and transfer to small river steamers.

With the lure of big money to be made, commercial and trading companies built warehouses to help with the transfer of goods and fleets of steamers to convey the "gold-crazed lunatics" and their freight up the Yukon.

Calling all steamships

The demand for steamships to carry passengers to the Klondike exploded. Ships were pulled off other routes to fill the need, and ships that had been out of service were quickly renovated and placed in the water. Anything that could float was used. Even old sailing ships had their masts removed and were converted into barges that were then towed by tug boats.

From the small *SS Dora*, a little more than 100 feet, to the *SS Athena*, a passenger steamer of around 365 feet, ships were pulled into

After miners discovered rich gold deposits along the Klondike, St. Michael became a shipbuilding hub where many companies, like the Northern Commercial Company seen in this photograph, set up shop.

Along with prospectors flooding into the tiny settlement of St. Michael, con men looking to make a quick buck also swarmed to the budding town. In an effort to stem the tide of scoundrels, the U.S. War Department built an army post, Fort St. Michael, set up a 100-mile reserve around it and ordered the "sure thing" men to leave.

service to carry stampeders and supplies. Propeller-driven steamships were the most common.

Overcrowding on ships heading to the Klondike was the general rule. Small steamers like the *SS Amur*, designed to carry 160 passengers, were outfitted with temporary quarters and carried as many as 500 passengers. Temporary quarters usually meant a bunk bed placed in the holds right next to temporary animal stalls.

And as the demand increased, the price went up from $10 to $20 before the stampede to as much as $50 for a one-way ticket from Seattle to Skagway. The Seattle waterfront became a mass of confusion as stampeders, well-wishers and tons of freight lined the docks waiting to be loaded for the trip north. More than 9,000 people and 36,000 tons of supplies left Seattle in the first six weeks after the *Portland* landed with the news of the Klondike strike in July 1897.

Ships assembled at St. Michael

The Northern Commercial Company and its rival, the North American Transportation and Trading Company, enlarged their facilities and built boats at a feverish pitch in St. Michael, too. New companies like the Alaska Exploration Company and the Seattle Yukon Transportation Company also sprang up.

Some of the companies shipped parts and pieces for boats on ocean liners headed north, and then men assembled the steamers, barges and tugs in St. Michael. As the gold rush wore on, river steamers were built in Seattle and gingerly made the 3,000-mile voyage on the open ocean under their own power. Some were towed by large ships.

Transportation opportunists weren't the only ones eyeing the potential for profits in St. Michael. Gangs of gamblers pitched tents along the beach and welcomed those passing through to try their hands at games of chance.

In an effort to dissuade the con men, the U.S. War Department built an army post, Fort St. Michael, and patrolled a 100-mile perim-

Con men often tried to unload prospectors' pokes by luring them into rigged activities, like the shell game pictured above.

eter. The commander of the post and his men kept a close eye on the "sure thing" men and professional gamblers.

All-water route

Although the all-water route, which started in Seattle and continued from St. Michael, was considered the easiest and most comfortable for those who had money, conditions on board most boats were crowded and filthy.

Advertised by the Alaska Commercial Company to cost $150 and take about one month to complete, most travelers found the claim to be an optimistic estimate. Not only did the price increase to about $2,000 at the height of the rush – close to $60,000 in modern money – storms and problems encountered navigating the Yukon River commonly turned the trip into a two-month-or-more ordeal.

Under optimum conditions, river steamers leaving St. Michael only could make 100 miles a day churning against the powerful current of the muddy Yukon. Running one-half to six miles per hour, it took more than two weeks for the boats to make the 1,700-mile trip to Dawson City and the Klondike.

But at the height of the stampede in late 1897, winter was setting in and many stampeders spent more than a year reaching the Klondike because their vessels became trapped in the frozen ice.

Of the 1,800 stampeders who chose this route, only 43 reached Dawson City, and of these, 35 had to turn back for lack of supplies, according to the "Milepost."

Many adventurers who chose not to travel the water route through St. Michael tackled their choice of two other land routes instead – the Chilkoot Pass and the White Pass trails.

21

WHITE PASS AND CHILKOOT PASS TRAILS

The two major land routes to the Klondike gold fields were the White Pass and Chilkoot Pass trails. The White Pass, named for one of Canada's ministers of the interior, appeared a less arduous trail over the mountains than the steep Chilkoot. It started at Skagway, and the first several miles of White Pass had good road with a gentle upward grade wide enough for pack animals. However, that road was followed by a series of narrow climbs on a rocky switchback path.

Thousands of pack animals died along the White Pass trail route in 1897.

Miners streamed into Skagway and then packed their 2,000-pound outfits of food, tools, clothes and other supplies to Dyea, pictured here, a camp located just before the ascent through the Chilkoot Pass.

White Pass eventually earned the name "Dead Horse Trail," because 3,000 pack animals died along the route in less than three months. A combination of "Klondicitis," a name given to the panic and rush when stampeders drove their animals hard to reach the Klondike before the next person, as well as inexperience, lack of proper food and poor trail conditions contributed to the high death toll.

By September 1897, officials closed the White Pass trail due to the horrible conditions and rotting horse flesh. And although some stampeders still managed to go that route, the White Pass and Yukon Route Railroad, constructed between 1898 and 1900, put an end to most use of the trail.

The 33-mile Chilkoot Pass trail, which started one mile from Dyea, just north of Skagway, also had steep, forbidding grades, but it turned out to be the most direct route to lakes Lindemann and Bennett, the headwaters of the Yukon. The trail had been a vital link in the trade network of the region, where the Tlingit Indians controlled the Chilkoot trail. They made annual trips from the coast carrying fish oil, clam shells and dried fish to trade with Interior Natives.

Thousands cross the Chilkoot Pass

Around 22,000 people attempted the trail in the fall of 1897, and a human chain stretched across the entire length of the pass. Those who paused to rest with their loads often had to wait hours to re-enter the line.

Newspapers, like The Chicago Record, printed lists of supplies needed by those seeking to travel to the northern gold fields. The papers stressed that based on reports of hundreds who had traveled to the placer mines of the Klondike region previously, each man would need enough food, clothing and working materials to last at least one year.

In order to get all 2,000 pounds of gear to the top, each Klondiker had to climb to the 3,739-foot summit of Chilkoot Pass dozens of times. The pass, located on the Alaska-Canada boundary, is 4.1 miles northeast of Mount Hoffman and 17 miles north of Skagway.

The Record's analysis showed that men who'd lived in Alaska among the gold-bearing creeks for anywhere from one to 10 years, figured that an adequate supply of food per day per man varied from 4-1/2 to 5-1/2 pounds. That brought the actual food supply for one person for one year to 1,600 pounds.

"Highly carbonaceous food should predominate; stimulants of alcoholic character should be avoided," the Record reported. "One pound of tea is equal to seven pounds of coffee for drinking purposes; three-quarters of an ounce of saccharin (this concentrated sweet can be obtained from druggists) is equal to twenty-five pounds of sugar, so that three ounces of saccharin is equal to 100 pounds of sugar. Citric acid is a remedy for scurvy."

The newspaper went on to list other essentials for a gold-seeker's outfit, including 150 pounds of bacon, 250 pounds of flour, 40 pounds of rice, matches, a gold pan, one tea pot and a whipsaw.

As the stampede north evolved, enterprising prospectors dreamed up horse-, gasoline- and steam-powered tramways that ran up to the summit of Chilkoot Pass. For a fee, miners could have their outfits lifted to the summit and save themselves 30-40 trips packing all their gear up the "Golden Staircase."

Many heading to the Klondike through Dyea Valley, like Mr. and Mr. Fred Card and their family, lugged their supplies on their backs and pulled homemade carts.

The estimated cost per outfit of food, clothing, hardware and medicine, of which one bottle of "good whiskey" was a part, came to about $140 if bought in Seattle. Those who waited to purchase their outfits in Alaska paid three to four times as much.

Packing supplies a problem for many

Compiling and paying for a complete 2,000-pound outfit may have been the easiest part of the equation. Hauling it up the Chilkoot Trail was another matter.

Once they reached Skagway or Dyea, many stampeders paid Native packers between 12 cents and $1 to carry their supplies. Others less fortunate had to make as many as 30 trips to shuttle their supplies across the pass, since they couldn't carry much more than 70 pounds at a time. The relay of supplies along the trail ballooned the hike to more than 1,000 miles.

The trail was so steep that 1,200 steps were cut into the ice and snow to prevent the stampeders from sliding down. One enterprising prospector also set up a horse-powered tram to hoist luggage between a point on the pass, known as the Scales, to the summit for a small fee in early autumn 1897. By the following spring, three gasoline- and steam-powered tramways operated and ran up and down the pass. If a stampeder could afford the 5 to 15 cents per pound fee, then buckets suspended on a cable carried his cargo to the summit.

Once they'd carried all their supplies up the "Golden Staircase" to the 3,739-foot summit of Chilkoot Pass, the stampeders continued on their way after paying a duty on their goods to the North West Mounted Police, forerunners of the Royal Canadian Mounted Police. The Mounties inspected each outfit to make sure the prospectors carried enough food, clothing and equipment to live safely for one year. Most outfits consisted of 1,200 pounds of food and 800 pounds of clothes and equipment.

City of Seattle

Stampeders, like these actresses heading to Dawson in 1897, had to ford the Dyea River along the Chilkoot Pass trail. They are, from left, Irene Stanky, May Biggs, Maude Earl (being carried), Lulu Johnson and Mrs. Jack Sullivan.

Oddities also cross the Chilkoot Trail

Stories from the gold-rush days hint that a prospector named Mike Mahoney climbed to the summit of Chilkoot Pass in 1898 with a piano strapped to his back.

As the story goes, Mahoney, who mined a claim in the Klondike, hopped aboard the *City of Seattle* and found it stuffed to the bulwark with passengers, freight and a variety of animals, including more than 100 dogs headed to Skagway on consignment and horses crowded into stalls in the dining room.

Mahoney shared his stateroom with a strange little man named Hal Henry, booking agent and manager of Henry's Theatrical Entertainers. At first Mahoney avoided the undersized fellow, but soon he became intrigued with Henry's wild plan to take six beautiful, musically talented sisters and their instruments to Dawson. Called the "Sunny Samson Sisters Sextette," Essie, Bessie, Tessie,

Nellie, Ethel and Maud brought their violins, trumpets, horns, clarinets, trombones, bull fiddle and piano with them on the ship.

Henry told Mahoney he was sure the miners would pay to see and hear the lovely creatures, according to "This was Klondike Fever" by Harold Merritt Stumer.

"Luxury goods, that's what brings in the money, and that's what my girls are," Henry said. "They're beautiful, they're talented, and they're personable, and those woman-hungry miners will pay anything to see them perform."

Mahoney agreed that the girls would be popular, but he questioned whether they knew the hazards that lay ahead on their journey to Dawson.

Tough trail ahead

Henry assured him that the girls had traveled all over the world, under all sorts of conditions, and he had no doubt they could cover the several hundred miles of frozen wilderness between Skagway and Dawson. But he wasn't so sure about the piano, wrote Stumer.

After a while, Mahoney started to believe in the theatrical manager and decided to help him out. He told Henry that he'd figure out how to get the piano over the pass.

"They say Skookum Jim toted a 200-pound load of bacon up the Chilkoot, and if he did, I'll get your piano over somehow," Mahoney said.

Once the *City of Seattle* docked in Skagway, Mahoney secured drivers and teams to carry the party's outfit. But no one would touch the unwieldy piano. So Mahoney decided to carry it himself.

He gave it a trial run the morning after arriving in Skagway, according to Stumer, who grew up in Dawson.

"Give me the heft of her 'til I see how much she weighs," Mahoney said to two drivers at the Northern Commercial Company warehouse. He then bent over, spread his feet and stretched out his arms behind him.

The drivers hoisted the piano onto Mahoney's back. The prospector then adjusted the weight and walked around a bit.

"Hell," he said, "any husky kid could pack that thing. With the right pack harness and a shoulder pad it ought to be a lead pipe cinch."

Piano carried in vain

Mahoney and his drivers ferried over to Dyea, where they lashed the piano to a sled and fell in with a long line of gold seekers who were using dogs, horses, mules, oxen, burrows and reindeer to pull sleds loaded with supplies up the trail, Stumer wrote. They traveled from the head of Lynn Canal up the Dyea River, over piles of glacial moraine to Sheep Camp, where the treacherous climb up the ice staircase to summit Chilkoot Pass began.

For more than 30 minutes Klondike Mike Mahoney waited for his chance to step into line with his oversized load on his back. Once he landed on the first ice step, he coordinated his pace with the swing of the piano and didn't break the rhythm except to rest a few times.

Once stampeders made it up the Chilkoot Pass trail, some as many as 30 times, they then had to wait in line for the North West Canadian Mounted Police to inspect their outfits and grant permission for passage into Canada.

At the top of the summit, he eased the piano down and then tied it to the sled that one of the drivers had carried up. He then harnessed the dogs, and within a couple hundred yards, was at the Canadian border.

A Mountie asked Mahoney what he had in the sled.

"A piano," Mahoney replied, and explained about the theatrical group and its plan to entertain miners in Dawson.

The officer told him no one would be permitted to take six women across the border. Mahoney argued in vain and finally returned to Skagway, where Henry had already received the news, Stumer wrote. Both men were somewhat relieved that they wouldn't be dragging six "helpless" females hundreds of miles to Dawson, and the partnership broke up amicably.

The piano remained at the top of the Chilkoot Pass for quite some time. It eventually ended up in a saloon in a town that sprang up between the passes and Lake Bennett.

Anna DeGraf crossed the Chilkoot Pass trail several times in search of her son.

The dance troupe performed for six months in the notorious Soapy Smith's honky-tonk, according to Alaska historian Lael Morgan in her book, "Good Time Girls," and the press reported they retained their modesty and virtue.

A mother's quest

A widowed German immigrant who traveled that arduous Chilkoot route carried a means to support herself: a sewing machine.

Anna DeGraf, who lost her husband in a gold-mining acci-

Anna DeGraf, who first climbed the Chilkoot Pass trail in 1894, searched in vain for her son who had come north looking for gold. She spent two years in Circle, Alaska, pictured here in 1896, sewing tents and making dresses for dancehall girls.

dent in the West, climbed the Chilkoot Trail in 1894 at the age of 53. She hoped to find her youngest son, George, who'd left for the gold-filled Yukon region six years earlier.

Wearing a heavy skirt, blouse, warm jacket, cap and sturdy boots, DeGraf hiked the trail on crutches while carrying her sewing machine and a feather bed. She later wrote:

"I was so impressed I felt I could never go on. Some of the party were impatient and wanted to push ahead. 'Oh, come on,' they said. 'We don't care about scenery, we want to find gold.'

"I exclaimed aloud, 'My God, how beautiful you have made the world!' We camped there overnight and the next morning started over the deep crevasses in the ice. One misstep might have sent us into oblivion."

When the widow heard that a man named DeGraf had passed through the Interior, she continued toward the Yukon to join her son.

Weather forced her to winter in Circle City, which had become the largest log cabin town in the world following a major gold discovery there in 1892. She found work sewing tents for the Alaska Commercial Company, owned by Jack McQuesten and his wife, Katherine.

Widow sews as she searches

DeGraf asked everyone she met if they had news of her son. She spent two winters in Circle City sewing tents, as well as dresses for dancehall girls, before selling her sewing machine and heading to San Francisco to be with her daughter.

She exchanged her gold dust for $1,200 cash, and in 1897, bought another sewing machine and bolts of fabric after hearing news of the Klondike strike. DeGraf went north again over the Chilkoot Trail, hoping to locate her son.

Once stampeders crossed the White Pass or Chilkoot Pass trails and made it to either Lake Lindemann or Lake Bennett, pictured here in 1898, they had to build boats to navigate 550 miles down the Yukon River to reach Dawson.

Ultimately DeGraf traveled north seven times. Along with Circle City, where she helped start the first school, her search took her to Dawson, Whitehorse, Skagway and Juneau. She supported herself with her sewing machine and befriended miners, dancehall girls, theater performers and Alaska Natives.

At the age of 78, she finally left for good after she learned about the birth of a great-granddaughter in San Francisco. She found employment as a wardrobe mistress with the Pantage's theater company in the Bay area and worked there until she turned 90 in 1929.

She died the following year never having heard from the son whose disappearance first sent her over the Chilkoot Trail.

Stampeders build boats

Once stampeders successfully climbed the Chilkoot Trail and passed muster with the Mounties, paid their duty and hiked on to Lake Bennett or Lake Lindemann, they then had to build boats to navigate 500-plus miles along the Yukon River to Dawson City.

Once they reached Dawson in 1899, most stampeders found the cost of living high and the good gold claims already taken. So many pitched tents along the waterfront and tried to sell their supplies to get money for the trip home.

The upper portions of the Yukon were navigable about five months out of the year, from late May into mid-October. Bad timing left several thousand people staring at frozen water once they'd hiked down from the summit in the fall of 1897. The stampeders had to hunker down and struggle to survive until the river thawed.

Those who'd hauled pieces of prefabricated boats over the trail spent time putting them together. Others quickly stripped the area of standing timber and constructed boats from scratch.

When the ice finally broke the following May, about 800 boats set sail for the Klondike, unaware of the rapids that awaited them. Ten people drowned and more than 150 boats wrecked in the first few days on the river.

The Mounties were quick to respond. They established specific regulations for boats going down the Yukon, specifying that only experienced pilots could navigate boats through difficult rapids and women and children had to walk around the rapids. The Mounties

Not only did prospectors face back-breaking days dragging their gear to the Klondike, they also had mundane chores to perform once they set up camp along the way.

also required a serial number be displayed on each boat. The Mounties recorded the numbers, as well as the names of the boats' occupants and addresses of next of kin, to expedite searches if boats failed to check in along the way.

Slim pickings once Dawson reached

Almost none of the 100,000 gold seekers who left for the Klondike in the fall of 1897 by way of the Stikine River Trail, White Pass Trail, the Chilkoot Pass Trail or the all-water route made it to Dawson by the winter. The few who did faced starvation in the ill-supplied town. Less than half reached Dawson by the following fall, and only a fraction of those who arrived still had the desire to look for gold.

Most of the land had been claimed by the time those stampeders got there, and they found living costs sky-high and mining tough. Only a fortunate few who had the financial capital to buy an existing claim, buy into a partnership or lease a claim had any chance of finding gold.

A mere handful of people made any money at all during the peak of the gold rush in 1897-1898, including Carmack, Berry and Charley Anderson, dubbed "The Lucky Swede," who purchased No. 29 Above Eldorado for $800. Anderson removed more than $1 million in less than four years.

22

TRAILS TO GOLD

Photo Essay

All-water Route

Stikine Route

White Pass Trail Route

Chilkoot Pass Trail Route

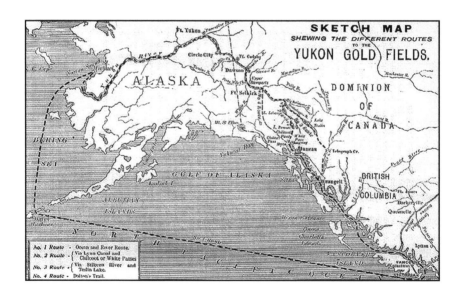

And they're on their way!

Steamships like the *Roanoke*, seen here disgorging the first-of-the-year gold-laden passengers from the Klondike in Seattle in 1898, carried stampeders back to Alaska ports in Wrangell, Skagway and St. Michael.

Those passengers dropped off at Wrangell took the lesser-traveled Stikine Trail to the Klondike gold fields through Whitehorse; stampeders who hopped off at Skagway climbed either the White Pass or Chilkoot Pass trails; and those who took steamers all the way to St. Michael transferred to smaller steamers to chug up the Yukon River to Dawson.

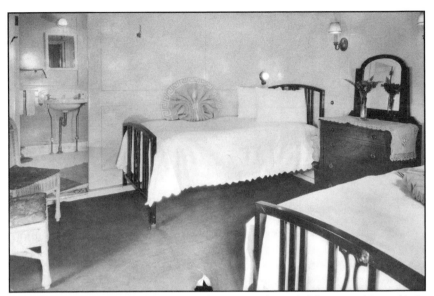

Above: Gold-rush adventurers who had money and traveled by steamship to Alaska could book passage in a deluxe stateroom, which looked similar to the one pictured onboard the S.S. Yukon.

Below: Sometimes Klondikers had to share space with horses, too, like the one being hoisted aboard this steamer.

RUSH TO THE KLONDIKE

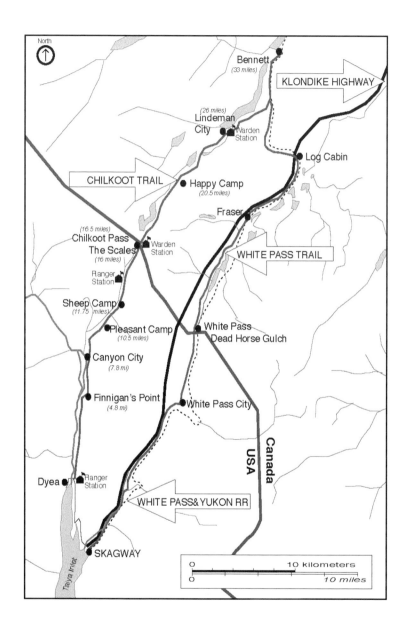

North

Bennett
(33 miles)

KLONDIKE HIGHWAY

(26 miles)
Lindeman
City
Warden
Station

Log Cabin

CHILKOOT TRAIL ● Happy Camp
(20.5 miles)

Fraser

(16.5 miles)
Chilkoot Pass
The Scales
(16 miles)
Warden
Station

WHITE PASS TRAIL

Ranger
Station

Sheep Camp
(11.75 miles)

●Pleasant Camp
(10.5 miles)

White Pass
Dead Horse Gulch

Canyon City
(7.8 mi)

Finnigan's Point
(4.8 mi)

●White Pass City

USA   Canada

Dyea ●   Ranger
Station

WHITE PASS&YUKON RR

● SKAGWAY

Taiya Inlet

0   10 kilometers
0   10 miles

The Stikine Trail

Stampeders traveling through Fort Wrangell, pictured here in 1897, headed for the Stikine River trail that led to Whitehorse. In the winter months, confined under a 10-foot layer of ice and snow, the river became a highway. Through frigid temperatures, Klondikers traversed this treacherous road, piggy-backing enormous packs about 300 feet, dropping them, and going back for more loads.

Above: A community developed as more and more Klondikers on their way to Dawson passed through Fort Wrangell, pictured here in 1897.

Below: Leaving Wrangell, prospectors then traveled the Stikine River route, which took them through the gold-rush town of Glenora, pictured here in the late 1800s.

Above: Once stampeders made it through the Stikine River trail, they had to build boats that could withstand the pounding and dangers of the Whitehorse Rapids.

Below: Wrecks were common. Klondikers in the picture below are drying out their loads after taking a spill on their way to the gold fields.

The White Pass Trail

Above: Skagway, which sits in a narrow glaciated valley at the head of the Taiya Inlet, was established as a result of the Klondike strike in Canada's Yukon Territory. Thousands of prospectors traveled through the Southeast Alaska town as they began the arduous 500-plus-mile journey to the gold fields via either the White Pass or Chilkoot Pass trails.

Below: Once they arrived in Skagway, shown here in 1897, many early stampeders loaded up pack horses and hauled their 2,000-pound outfits up the trails.

Above: Stampeders on their way to the Klondike struggled with horses pulling outfits loaded on sleds along the White Pass trail in 1898. The summit, which is 2,900 feet high, is about 13 miles northeast of Skagway.

RUSH TO THE KLONDIKE

Lower left: Stampeders could pay $1 for a meal at Hungry Man's Retreat restaurant at Porcupine Creek on the White Pass trail in 1897. In "En Route to the Klondike," photographer Frank LaRoche wrote:

"This is a restaurant in the wilderness where you pay a dollar a meal and frequently get something you are not looking for. Yet one's appetite is such after these weary marches that anything is eaten with relish, particularly if a little fresh meat is included. The most prevalent trouble in this part is scurvy, which is the result of a scarcity of vegetables and fresh meat. A diet of beans, salt pork and bad bacon with flour at $50 a sack brings trouble; and a restaurant in the wilderness is a very welcome spectacle even if one does have to pay a dollar for a four-ounce steak."

Below: The White Pass and the Chilkoot Pass trails were the two major land routes to the Klondike gold fields. The White Pass appeared a less arduous route over the mountains than the steep Chilkoot Pass but had a series of narrow climbs on a rocky switchback path.

It became known as "Dead Horse Trail," because 3,000 pack animals died along the route in less than three months. By September 1897, officials closed the White Pass trail due to the horrible conditions and rotting horse flesh, although some prospectors still used the trail.

Prospectors traveling the White Pass Trail ended up at Lake Bennett where they had to build boats to travel the remainder of the 500-plus-mile trip down the dangerous Yukon River to Dawson. A small town grew up in the area surrounding the lake.

FIRST PASSENGER TRAIN OVER WHITE PASS AND YUKON ROUTE TO SUMMIT OF WHITE PASS, FEB. 20 1899.
CROSSING EAST FORK OF SKAGUAY RIVER

While some stampeders still managed to head to the Klondike gold fields by way of the White Pass trail after it was closed in September 1897, the White Pass and Yukon Route Railroad built between 1898 and 1900 put an end to most use of that trail. This photo shows the first passenger train crossing a trestle bridge along the east fork of Skagway River on Feb. 20, 1899.

The Chilkoot Pass Trail

The majority of stampeders heading to the Klondike chose the Chilkoot Pass Trail that started at Dyea, pictured here, located at the head of Lynn Canal. Once gold-seekers left Dyea, about five miles north of Skagway, they had the 3,739-foot-high Chilkoot Pass summit to reach, and then they faced a long hike to Lake Lindemann.

These men are fording Dyea River for a second time with a cart full of supplies in 1897. Photographer Frank LaRoche gives an account of what the experience was like in "En Route to the Klondike:"

"At the second crossing, about one mile and a half above the first, these men are crossing with perhaps 1,000 pounds of provisions. In September the river here was not far from 100 feet wide and 18 inches deep. In spring the melting snow sometimes increases the depth of the water to four feet or more, when a ferry is used as at the first crossing. Here, a party of five are northbound, crossing and re-crossing with this cart until all their supplies are over, while two packers with horses are returning south after other loads. Long rubber boots protect them from the water, while a complete outfit appears upon the cart, so that they can pitch their tents wherever circumstances demand."

Those traveling along the Chilkoot Pass trail in 1897 didn't have an easy time. Photographer Frank LaRoche gives us a glimpse into what it was like to hand-carry pieces of a boat to Lake Lindemann.

"A trying climb on Dyea Trail. Mile after mile of such broken railway and uncertain footing is met with en route to the mountain top. The photographer was shown the toilsome march of the pack train bearing supplies for the miners. At the moment this photograph was taken, a fallen horse in front of the line had compelled all behind it to stop until the animal was assisted to regain its feet. In this picture can be seen two men carrying a section of a boat. Later, even this light load became too great to be borne up the mountainside, and they were compelled to saw it in two pieces and divide the burden. On reaching the shores of the lake, the pieces of the boat were patched together again."

The three men and dog in this photograph are eating a meal inside a cabin in Sheep Creek in 1898 – probably filling up before beginning the ascent to the summit.

Upper left: Sheep Camp was a main stopping point along the Dyea Trail that led to the Chilkoot Pass summit. Jack London and fellow travelers Jim Goodman, Fred Thompson and Martin Tarwater are among those pictured here on Sheep Camp's Front Street in 1897.

"This is the principal camp on the Dyea Trail," wrote photographer Frank LaRoche in his account "En Route to the Klondike," written in 1898. "In August and September there were 1,000 or more people encamped here. The log structure on the left was the leading hotel where you might eat for 75 cents and sleep on the floor for 50 cents, if you furnished your own bedding. Beyond here a meal could not be had at any price. This is right on the edge of what is known as the timber line. Thence to the other side is about 10 miles. In all the district there is not sufficient wood to heat a cup of coffee, so you are obliged to carry your own wood or you want to camp within that distance."

Sheep Camp was the last "city" before the Chilkoot Pass and was packed with thousands of stampeders, especially when the weather turned bad and made travel slow. At the height of the gold rush to the Yukon, it boasted 16 hotels, 14 restaurants, three saloons and two dancehalls.

Below: Once prospectors left Sheep Camp, the next stop was the base of the Chilkoot Pass. Shortly after the initial rush, enterprising stampeders rigged an aerial tramway to haul prospectors' supplies up to the summit of the Chilkoot Pass trail for a fee. Most prospectors didn't have any money to spare, however, and hauled their own outfits up the trail or hired Native packers for between 12 cents and $1 a load.

Some Klondikers and Native packers rest while others make their way up the rocky path toward The Scales on their way to the Chilkoot Pass summit in 1897.

Too tired to go any farther, stampeders pitched tents at the approach to Chilkoot Pass in 1897. Frank LaRoche describes the scene.

"Forty-five degrees incline and summit of Chilkoot Pass. This is the most difficult and dreaded portion of the journey, the trail rising here eleven feet in half a mile over a perfect maze of broken rock. In this photograph may be seen an almost continuous line of white specks reaching to the depression at the summit. Each is a human being with a pack upon his back toiling slowly upward. Toward the summit is a sheer ascent of 1,000 feet, where a slip would certainly be fatal."

View showing the mode of travel on the Chilkoot.

A Klondiker pauses and watches as other stampeders head up the trail to the summit of Chilkoot Pass carrying outfits comprised of items like a sled, shovel, axe, tent, blankets, cooking utensils and a 7-foot whipsaw for sawing logs into lumber, as well as other tools for building a boat.

These hardy souls also carried grub to keep them alive for several months as the country along the trail provided nothing. Staples included flour, dried beans and sow belly. Evaporated prunes and apricots helped to prevent scurvy.

And the stampeders carried gold pans. In addition to its use in washing out gold from creeks, the gold pan also served as a dish pan, washing bowl, mixing pan for sourdough bread and baking tin for the same.

Several trips were necessary as a strong man could not carry more than 70-80 pounds on his back at a time. After depositing a load at the top, the Klondikers slid downhill through the snow to get the next load.

The first known crossing of this pass by a white man was made around 1864 by an employee of the Hudson's Bay Company, who started at Fort Selkirk and was delivered by the Chilkoot Indians to Capt. Swandson, commander of one of the company's steamers.

RUSH TO THE KLONDIKE

Above left: Thousands of stampeders with hopes of making it rich in the Klondike ascended Chilkoot Pass in 1898. But Klondikers had to take care crossing the Chilkoot Pass during the winter. Stampeders struggled in blizzards, snow, frigid temperatures and avalanches. The 26-mile trail over Chilkoot Pass was steep and hazardous and the trail shot up about 1,000 feet in the final half mile. Travelers did not always fare better in the summer, however, as stampeders struggled in rain and fog over giant boulders and bogs.

To move one outfit over the pass, stampeders packed and cached their goods up to 40 times, and the terrain on the last four miles of the trail was too rough for pack animals. Discarded supplies littered the trail as stampeders cast unnecessary items aside. Many took three months to move their goods from Dyea to the summit.

Bottom left: Prospectors recover from an avalanche on April 3, 1898. A storm deposited heavy, deep, soft snow on the pass and then several warm days made perfect conditions for the major avalanche.

Above: Stampeders dig the dead out from underneath the mountain of snow that tumbled down from the summit in April 1898.

After stampeders made it to the summit of Chilkoot Pass, they had to lay down their loads, mark their spots and head back down for another load. Once all supplies were hauled to the top, the miners then hiked another 13 miles to Lake Lindemann or on to Lake Bennett, another four miles, where they built boats to navigate the Yukon River.

Klondikers had to pass inspection with the North West Canadian Mounted Police, who inspected each outfit to make sure that everyone who crossed over into Canada had the required 1-ton of provisions.

Once stampeders reached the summit of Chilkoot Pass, they then had to carry and drag tons of provisions over the harsh paths down to either Lake Bennett, above, which also was the terminus of the White Pass Trail, or Lake Lindemann, below. The crowd of Klondikers then waited until the river ice broke up so they could float down the Yukon into Dawson.

Many who stayed at Lake Lindemann regretted their decision in the spring because ice and snow had hidden the wild rapids between Lake Lindemann and Lake Bennett. What would have been a tedious but safe journey in the winter turned into a short but dangerous navigation through churning rapids in the spring.

Many Klondikers who made it to Lake Lindemann or Lake Bennett found the lakes frozen over, so they spent the winter whipsawing lumber and making boats that could traverse the Yukon River in the spring.

Above: Canyon City sat at the upstream end of the canyon and was the place where most people stopped to plan their next moves. Many unloaded their boats and laboriously portaged their goods. A few attempted to run their boats through the raging waters.

By June 1898, a huge bottleneck had developed at Canyon City, but while nearly 300 boats had wrecked in the rapids, only five people had drowned. North West Mounted Police Inspector Samuel Steele confessed, "Why more casualties have not occurred is a mystery to me." In an attempt to prevent any more casualties, Steele issued an order that skilled pilots had to be hired to take boats through.

An eight-kilometer tramway was built on the east bank of the river that ran from Canyon City to the foot of the rapids, just across from present-day Whitehorse. It hauled goods on horse-drawn cars for 3 cents per pound. A rival tram, built on the west bank of the river, soon competed with the first.

Although a small settlement developed at Canyon City, there was no reason for its existence once the railroad was completed to Whitehorse.

Bottom left: Miners who chose to winter at Lake Lindemann had to navigate their boats through the rapids of One Mile River to reach Lake Bennett, where they then began their journey down the Yukon River to Dawson.

From Whitehorse, those seeking gold in the Klondike traveled by horse, dog sled and any other means possible to reach Dawson. And prospectors hiking to the Klondike often took time out to check creeks for colors.

Men on the forward deck of the Yukon River steamer *White Horse* guide a cable as it passes around a capstan. The paddle wheeler is negotiating the narrow Five Finger Rapids on its way to Dawson.

The steamboat *Monarch* arrives at Dawson, Yukon Territory, on July 21, 1898, loaded with prospectors eager to seek out the gold fields of the Klondike. Prospectors who finally made it to Dawson – by way of the all-water, the White Pass, the Chilkoot Pass or Stikine routes – found the settlement, shown here in 1899, blossoming in the wilderness. However, they also found the cost of living high and most of the good land claimed, so many turned around and went back home.

Dawson had plenty of dancehalls, saloons and brothels. It had tons of gold, vats of whisky, and it had gamblers and 'scarlet women.' A period of chaos lasted for a few months in 1898, then constables of the North West Mounted Police, earning $1.25 a day, came to town and maintained law and order through the rush.

RUSH TO THE KLONDIKE

Gold seekers who finally reached Dawson often found the cost of living too high and the best land already claimed. Disappointed, they sold their outfits along the Dawson water-front as those pictured above and below are trying to do in 1898.

Stampeders struggle in the Klondike

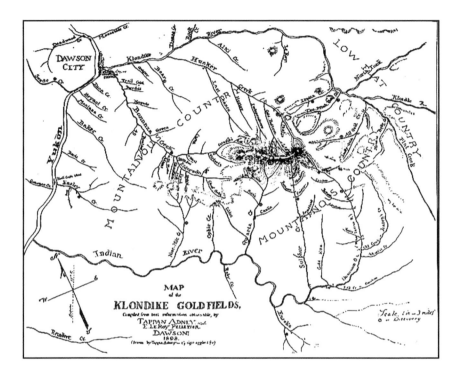

This map of the Klondike gold fields was compiled from the best information obtainable by Tappan Adney and E. LeRoy Pelletier in 1898. It resulted after George Washington Carmack and his Native companions, Dawson Charley and Skookum Jim, explored the area around the Klondike River. The three lucky prospectors discovered gold on Bonanza Creek on Aug. 17, 1896. A short time later, at the nearby mining camp of Fortymile, Carmack registered the discovery claim. Within days, Bonanza and Eldorado creeks had been staked from end to end.

Thousands of pick-and-shovel miners, prospectors, storekeepers, saloon keepers, bankers, gamblers, prostitutes and con men from every corner of the continent poured through snow-choked mountain passes and down the Yukon River to stake their claims to fortune on both Bonanza and Eldorado creeks, as well as creeks with names like Last Chance and Too Much Gold.

Most seekers found no gold at all. But the prospect of sudden riches was not all that mattered. For many of those who made the incredible journey, the Klondike represented escape from the humdrum and an adventure into a new frontier.

Once Klondikers made it to the gold fields, many whipsawed logs to build cabins, like the one pictured below.

Above: Miners built interesting dwellings along their route to riches, including this house made of bottles at the White Pass Summit.

Above: Some miners, like those in the the photograph above, brought their diggings inside their cabins and continued panning for the shining metal in the warmth of their abodes.

Lower left: Miners often worked the sluice boxes they built in the gold-rich fields of the Klondike region during the late 1890s and early 1900s. A sluice is a long trough-like box set on a slope through which placer gravel is carried by a stream of water. The sand and gravel are carried away, while most of the gold and other heavy minerals are caught in riffles or a blanket on the floor.

Right: Many Klondikers traveled to Dawson and shopped on Front Street to resupply their outfits before heading back to the gold diggings to work their claims.

Above: Frost at the entrance to a tunnel in a placer gold mine in the Yukon Territory around 1899 attests to the fact that prospectors had to work in less-than-favorable conditions during the winter months.

Left: This 1897 original drawing by Knight and Noble-Ives, titled "Gold Miners at Work," appeared in the book, "Klondike: A Manual for Goldseekers," and shows how gold miners heated the earth to thaw the ground so they could dig down to bedrock to find gold.

PHOTO BY F.H. NOWELL
1980   FREE FERRY ACROSS KLONDIKE

Billed as a "free ferry," this tramline ferried people and goods across the Klondike River south of Dawson, Yukon Territory, around 1898.

Dawson City grew out of a marshy swamp near the confluence of the Yukon and Klondike rivers. In two years it became the largest city in Canada west of Winnipeg with a population that fluctuated between 30,000 and 40,000 people.

By the summer of 1898, the carnival atmosphere gave way to the raw reality of heat, mosquitoes, mud, filth, stench and disease. Horses got stuck in the muck of the streets and wagons sank up to their axles. Pedestrians waded knee-deep through what writer T.C. Down described as "this festering mass of putrid muskeg."

Typhoid broke out in July and was rampant throughout the summer. The town's two small hospitals were filled to capacity.

Deathtrap in the Ice

Diabolical natural conditions cause hole in Yukon Ice
– Reported in the Dawson Daily News, Feb. 16, 1906

George H. Finnegan, a woodsman on the lower river, is in Dawson on business and brings a detailed description of the ice trap which probably carried to death and destruction the entire Sinclair party of Dawsonites on the 26th day of last October.

Mr. Finnegan's description of conditions at the jam, of the jam half broken, narrowing the current into a torrent, ending in a vast maelstrom which sucked down vast cakes of ice, is vivid and striking. He said:

"Had the devil and all his imps enlisted all the powers of nature to construct and maintain an absolutely invincible deathtrap, they could not have done better than at Cliff Creek just prior to the arrival there of the Dawson party in their scow.

I and a party of choppers camped on the scene the night of the 27th, and so diabolically perfect was the natural trap, we explored it thoroughly by daylight.

Let me describe it to you if I can, for I and my companions at that time remarked that never had we seen anything so deathlike, so invincible, so certain. Nothing made by man could have survived had it been caught anywhere within three miles of the last end of the trap.

Let me explain then that at Cliff Creek the Yukon narrows. Along about the 20th I should judge there had been a terrible jam just below the narrows. The ice had been caught and piled further and further up the river reaching finally to a point three miles above the narrows I speak of. Then this collision of ice had given way, but not the real jam, the accumulated water and ice finding an outlet under the center of the jam.

The result was diabolical. We explored every inch. Here is what any boat would find in passing down the river. Three miles above the jam it would be observed that the river commenced to rapidly narrow; sheer walls of ice, 15 to 20 feet high, had appeared, the current flowing steadily between. Not a thing to indicate that the deathtrap had been entered and that death was now as certain as if the axe had fallen. Gradually, without a break, the walls pinched together, in the form of an elongated V, like Miles Canyon, only infinitely worse, for men have been known to climb out of the canyon, but nothing could land in that V trap and climb out. Nor would there be any indication of the terrible danger ahead – none whatever, for the appearance was as if some jam had given way and gone down river, leaving a lane of open water. The bend at the narrows concealed everything, and even diverted the ominous sounds. Gradually the water grew swifter and the V got narrower. Evidently the towering ice walls were grounded, and absolutely confined the water. When I stood on top of that chasm and looked down at the foaming waters, it was like looking down a well.

The last mile of the trap rushed like a millrace. Natural canyons are nothing in comparison. The V ended at the jam proper, in a whirlpool 60 feet across. Into

RUSH TO THE KLONDIKE

this whirlpool the crazy current dashed and went down. Vast cakes of ice ran into it with the speed of a railway train, upended in an instant, and passed beneath the jam, to reappear in three-quarters of a mile all churned and ground into the finest of mush. The whole river dashed beneath the jam at this point, and nothing afloat could have hesitated an instant in taking the inevitable plunge.

Not a thing struck the jam, for the whirlpool could not be crossed. In fact, it was not a whirlpool, but a hole in the river, down which everything rushed with a frightful velocity. Even the water, when it reappeared just beyond the jam, was just foam.

I don't know that the Sinclair party met its fate there – nobody knows. This I know. If that scow entered that gorge three miles above the pool, it went down that hole in the water with every soul aboard. Not a dog could have escaped. The party left Dawson the 25th. I was in the jam on the 27th, and the indications were that the conditions I say had been the same for several days. I knew of no wreck when I was there, but myself and companions were struck with the infernal ingenuity with which nature had fashioned that deathtrap, and remarked it and explored it. A steamer would have gone down that hole in the water just as certainly. Nothing could have bucked the current, made fast to the icy sides of the gorge or have made a landing on the top of it."

Giant icebergs flowed down the Yukon River during spring breakup and caused hazardous conditions to traveling stampeders.

23

JACK DALTON BUILDS TOLL ROAD

The short, feisty, stocky frontiersman aimed a rifle at the party trying to travel over his Yukon trail without paying the toll. Jack Dalton meant business, and people found he was a tough man with whom to tangle. Dalton watched the group with their herd of cattle floundering through scrub trees and bushes and kept alongside for 300 miles to make sure they didn't set foot on his right of way.

The Dalton trail, named after the father of James Dalton whose name has been given to the North Slope Haul Road, opened a route in the 1890s from Pyramid Harbor on the Lynn Canal in Southeastern Alaska to the Yukon. It served a very useful purpose in the gold rush days. About 2,000 beef cattle successfully traveled it – a welcome addition to the miners' food supply.

In later years, the trail would become part of the Haines Highway. As one rides the road in relative comfort nowadays, one can hardly realize how the pioneers traveled in toil and sweat – saddle-sore horses and foot-sore men made the 300-mile trek.

Back in 1891 Jack Dalton and his traveling companion, E.J. Glave of the Leslie Exploration Expedition, decided "defective transportation is the sole reason for the undeveloped state of the land." Dalton, a rugged entrepreneur, had an important role in remedying the situation.

Jack Dalton, a feisty man who arrived in Alaska in the 1880s, became a member of Lt. Frederick Schwatka's exploration party and established a toll road to the Yukon gold fields based on his travels.

Dalton the adventurer

Born for adventure, danger and confrontations, Dalton first saw the light of day on the Cherokee Strip in 1855. Before coming to Alaska he spent a few years in Oregon as a logger and cowboy. Some shooting scrapes, however, made it expedient to leave that part of the country and he shipped out on a sailing vessel to Alaska.

It is reported that in 1884 he and other members of the crew spent a year in the Sitka jail for seal poaching. Another source said his ship wintered at Herschel Island in 1885.

He left the sea in 1886 and became a member of Lt. Frederick Schwatka's exploration party to Mount Saint Elias. Later he signed up with the Leslie party to explore the Interior and write reports for the Frank Leslie Illustrated Newspaper of New York.

That's when he met up with Glave, an English explorer who had been with Henry M. Stanley in Africa. He and Dalton developed mutual respect.

"Dalton," Glave wrote later, "is a most desirable partner – has excellent judgment, cool and deliberate in times of danger and possessed of great tact in dealing with the Indians ... as a camp cook, I've never seen his equal."

Dalton's ability to deal with the Indians was very helpful, for this was Indian country they were traversing. Indians had followed game trails in the vicinity and the proud and warlike Chilkats dominated trade. They never allowed the Interior Indians direct contact with white people.

A toll road established by Jack Dalton was the only toll road to endure, according to Pierre Berton, author of "Klondike Fever." Dalton laid out the trail following routes he had traversed with English explorer E.J. Glave of the Leslie Exploration Expedition in the early 1890s.

Dalton scopes out trail to Yukon

When Glave and Dalton were on their expeditions, the Indians tried to discourage them with tales of mighty glaciers and raging rivers, for success would wrest from the Chilkats control of the gate to the Interior. But Glave and Dalton were undaunted.

On their first trip, they started in the Interior and descended the turbulent Alsek River to the sea. Next time they started from the Chilkat village of Klukwan on the coast. On their first trip they had decided that the use of horses was practical and used them the second trip, as well. They finally arrived at Lake Kluane in Canada; then came the return to the coast, following the same route as that of their inward journey, riding horses most of the way.

Glave was never to return to the North; he was killed in another expedition to the Congo. But Dalton, in 1896, established a pack trail to the Yukon, partly following the 1891 route. The Klondike gold rush would find him prepared, and the Dalton Trail became an important gateway to the gold fields.

According to Pierre Berton, author of "Klondike Fever," Dalton was a respected figure in Dawson. Others had tried to establish a toll road, but Dalton was the only one to make it work. He was a hard man to get the better of, and once beat a man to a pulp for trying to establish a saloon on his property. He shot another for attempting to set the Indians against him, but he was acquitted.

Dalton later had a hand in establishing a route to get coal out of the Matanuska area, but that story is for another volume of Aunt Phil's Trunk.

Sea Captains, Scoundrels and Nuns

24

Sea captain stifles mutiny

When news reached Seattle of gold discoveries in Cook Inlet in 1896, every available vessel was pressed into service. With ships scarce, those heading north were filled to capacity with prospectors and their supplies.

Capt. Johnny O'Brien's steamship *Utopia*, which set out with 100 passengers that spring, was no different. In early May, it arrived close to Kachemak Bay, but couldn't continue up Turnagain Arm because of ice in Cook Inlet.

Although this turn of events didn't really bother the captain, he had no way of knowing that he soon would be teetering on the brink of death and his crew would be close to mutiny.

O'Brien was used to adventure, according to Mary J. Barry in her book, "A History of Mining on the Kenai Peninsula, Alaska." Born in Ireland in 1851, he'd been shanghaied at 16 while traveling home from engineering school in England and sailed around the world for six years. When he finally worked his way back to Ireland, he discovered his parents had died.

Sometime later, authorities arrested childhood friend Peter Mathews as a member of the Fenians and sentenced him to death. O'Brien and members of the Sinn Fein blew up the jail and rescued Mathews.

O'Brien shanghaied again

The two young men then escaped to the United States where O'Brien studied navigation. While in New York City, the two friends found themselves shanghaied onto the ship *Hampton*, which was to carry them to England to face trial as revolutionaries.

The men managed to escape, but knowing they could never return to Ireland, they decided to search for gold instead. The long-time friends unsuccessfully prospected in British Columbia in 1894, where a hungry Mathews died during a long, cold winter.

O'Brien returned to the sea. Over time, he made captain. And even though he had a couple of wrecks, he always stayed with his damaged ships. That helped him establish a reputation for tenacity and toughness.

He soon would have to rely on that toughness as he waited near Homer for the ice in Kachemak Bay to clear.

As several of his passengers jumped ship and made other arrangements to get to the gold fields in Cook Inlet, O'Brien suffered an attack of acute appendicitis and fell desperately ill.

After gold was discovered in Cook Inlet, steamships like the one pictured here plied the waters from Seattle to Kachemak Bay and dropped prospectors off near near Homer.

When Capt. Johnny O'Brien needed to have his appendix removed, Della Murray Banks, a Denver newspaperwoman who lived on the Homer Spit, pictured here in 1899, offered her house for the operation.

One of the remaining prospectors on board the *Utopia* told the captain that he'd once had a medical practice, but he did not divulge the reason that he'd abandoned it in favor of back-breaking work in Alaska's gold fields.

Mystery passenger watches over sea captain

Volunteers cleared out the galley home of Della Murray Banks, a Denver newspaperwoman who lived on the Homer Spit, for the operation. The doctor-turned-prospector, who hadn't performed an operation in years, accepted a fee of $1,000 and liberally dosed the captain with whiskey, the only anesthetic available.

And while the captain watched, the former doctor used a kitchen knife and scissors to remove the appendix and a forecastle needle and thread to suture the wound.

Even the doctor didn't expect the captain to make a full recovery. But under the watchful eye of a pleasant, well-mannered, dark-haired man named Mr. Smith, O'Brien emerged from his semiconscious condition seven days later and walked shakily onto the *Utopia* with the help of Smith and a sailor.

Since his passengers had departed or made other arrangements to get to Cook Inlet, O'Brien ordered his crew to turn the ship around and head back to Seattle.

After O'Brien watched his ship round Cape Elizabeth, he fell into a deep sleep in his bunk. He awoke four hours later to discover her sitting still.

Crew begins to mutiny

When he looked out his window and saw land all around, O'Brien picked up a medicine bottle and heaved it at the window to attract attention. The shattering glass brought a sailor to his cabin.

The sailor told the captain that his crew refused to continue the trip because the cook was bad.

O'Brien summoned Smith, according to Barry, and asked him for his two revolvers and help getting into a chair on deck. The captain then called for his crew.

As he pointed one revolver at the chief engineer's head, and the other at anyone who might interfere, O'Brien asked, "Are you going to turn the engines over and get the ship under way?"

The crew quickly changed its tune and headed the *Utopia* toward Seattle. It wasn't until much later that O'Brien learned the identity of the man known as Smith who'd helped him quash the mutiny and had nursed him back to health.

It was none other than the notorious confidence man, Jefferson Randolph Smith, better known to Alaskans as "Soapy."

Smith had traveled to Cook Inlet on the *Lakme*, but quickly learned that the area was not suitable for his "special talents." He headed to the Klondike the following year.

A man traveling to Cook Inlet volunteered to nurse *Utopia* Capt. Johnny O'Brien back to health following an operation to remove his appendix. That mystery man turned out to be none other than Jefferson Randolph Smith, better known to Alaskans as "Soapy," shown here a year later in his saloon, Peiser, in Skagway. After Soapy realized that Cook Inlet didn't have the population necessary for his shady games, he headed to the town at the beginning of the Chilkoot Pass Trail.

25

SOAPY SMITH HEADS TO SKAGWAY

The stream of gold pouring through the trails along the Klondike drew birds of prey like Soapy Smith as well as prospectors. Born Jefferson Randolph Smith, the intelligent and skilled criminal controlled a well-organized gang of thieves, thugs and con men during the heyday of the gold rush.

Soapy gained initial infamy in Denver, Colo., where he made a fortune from a soap scam. He'd wrap a $100 bill around a bar of soap and slap his own label around that bar. He then mixed his "special" soap in a box with numerous other bars, all bearing the name of his new product "Sapolion."

Soapy would walk into a local saloon where a silent partner "bought" a "randomly" selected bar for $5. Soapy's sales escalated at a phenomenal rate, but oddly enough, other $100 bars of soap rarely surfaced.

Soapy sailed north to mine the miners in Alaska after law enforcement suggested it might be better for his health if he left Colorado. Smith's northern operations extended from the ships plying the Inside Passage to the summits of the White Pass and Chilkoot Pass trails. His gang members posed as helpful fellow travelers who offered assistance and information to stampeders.

Soapy's shifty ways pad his pockets

Once his cohorts located the fattest wallets, they steered them to Soapy's bogus business operations and tents offering shell-game tables and phony poker games.

Soapy made his way to Skagway in the busy summer of 1897, where he moved from petty swindles to controlling most of Skagway's darker vices. He built a saloon-casino called Jeff's Place, and by January 1898, he was the uncrowned king of Skagway's underworld.

Few men walked out of Soapy's casino with more money than they brought in. And those who did, often met up with some of Soapy's "helpers" in Skagway's back alleys. The helpers helped themselves to the winnings.

One of Soapy's more ingenious schemes to lighten prospectors' pokes revolved around the telegraph office. Soapy himself oversaw

When Jefferson Randolph Smith, better known as "Soapy," arrived in Skagway in 1897, the town was filled with prospectors heading into the Klondike in search of riches or heading back out of Alaska with gold-filled pokes. Soapy made it his mission to lighten their loads and line his own pockets.

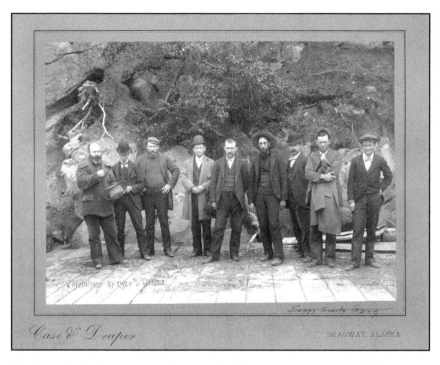

The Soapy Smith Gang terrorized the people of Skagway during the late 1890s.

the building of the office, which opened less than a week after construction began.

Miners came into the office to telegraph news of their strikes to folks back home. A few hours later, a telegraphed reply came back – usually asking the prospectors to send money. The helpful telegraph employees happily wired the miners' gold dust in return. There was only one problem. The telegraph wires extended only a few feet into Skagway's harbor.

Skagway residents tire of Soapy's antics

A committee of Skagway residents finally organized a group to run Soapy and his gang out of town. But Soapy retaliated and took over. He paid or coerced 300 residents to form a committee called the Law and Order Society of 317 Members.

By March 1898, Soapy Smith had caused conditions in the Southeast Alaska town to become unbearable. He and his gang controlled the town.

A meeting of citizens was called to discuss the murder of a miner named H. Bean, as well as other crimes, which resulted in 101 citizens issuing a warning to "all confidence, bunko, and sure-thing men to leave Skagway."

Soapy's followers replied in defiance.

Honest citizens held more meetings, some of which were packed by members of Soapy's gang who'd been informed of the get-togethers by traitors for the underworld cause.

The climax came on July 7 when a miner named J.D. Stewart staggered into Skagway with nearly $3,000 in gold. He first stored it in a hotel safe. But Soapy's henchmen convinced him to transfer it to Soapy's casino, where it disappeared during a staged brawl.

Soapy meets his match

The Committee of 101 called a meeting on the dock on July 8, 1898, and placed Frank H. Reid to guard the entrance to the long viaduct so that no unwanted intruders could attend. Reid, a quiet and determined fellow, was said to be the only man in Skagway that Soapy feared. He stood his ground as Soapy and his gang, who had heard about the meeting and decided to "crash" the party, rushed past a few unarmed men.

Reid, who had a pistol in his pocket, told Soapy to stop.

Soapy, who had a grudge against Reid, struck him with the butt of his Winchester.

Reid blocked the swing and fired. The cartridge missed.

Soapy swung his rifle toward Reid and fired.

At the same instant another bolt of fire flashed from Reid's revolver. An eyewitness stated that it looked as though they were spitting fire at each other.

Both men crumpled onto the planking, and as Reid fell, he fired again. Within seconds, Soapy lay dead, with a ball through his heart and another through his thigh. Reid lay mortally wounded from a

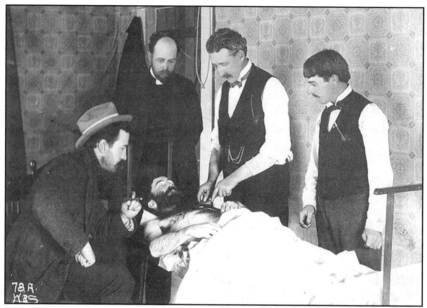

After Frank Reid killed Soapy Smith, pictured here on a gurney in an undertaker's office, Soapy's gang members took to their heels and headed out of town.

A posse formed and searched for the outlaws. One by one they were captured and arrested. So ended one of the most lawless eras of Skagway's history.

rifle ball that crashed through his groin. He died 12 days later and is buried in Skagway's cemetery. His headstone reads: "He gave his life for the Honor of Skagway."

26

MINERS STAMPEDE TO NOME

America's last big placer gold rush came in 1898, when gold was discovered at Cape Nome by three greenhorn Scandinavians.

Scandinavians John Brynteson, left, Jafet Lindberg, top, and Eric Lindblom, right, are credited with discovering gold at Cape Nome in 1898.

Swedish tailor Eric Lindblom, 41, who worked his way north as a deckhand on a whaling ship, Norwegian Jafet Lindberg, 24, who got free passage by pretending to be an experienced reindeer herder, and Swedish coal miner John Brynteson, 27, all ended up in Nome because the promising land in the Klondike already had been claimed.

Their Anvil Creek discovery yielded $3.5 million in gold by 1900, and during the next two decades, it brought in

Above: The scene that met prospectors' eyes as they disembarked from steamships off shore of Nome on Sept. 21, 1899, included driftwood, lumber, tents and frame buildings along the beach. Nome was just two months old.

Below: Along with tents and frame houses, miners also built shelters out of logs and sod along Nome's beach.

By July 25, 1900, Nome was a busy place with tents pitched on its beach as far as one could see.

another $80 million. The Nome stampede gave amateurs a chance to make fortunes, as well as provided a second chance to prospectors who'd failed elsewhere.

Following the Scandinavians' find, thousands of people left Dawson and headed to Nome. The town filled with shady characters and hardened criminals who didn't pay much attention to American mining laws. By July 1899, almost every potentially valuable claim had been jumped at least twice and some had multiple claimants.

Confusion and unrest reigned among the community's 3,000 residents. Until a soldier, assigned to a small detachment sent up from St. Michael to guard the settlement, and an old prospector from Idaho found gold in the sands of Nome's beaches.

Gold-filled beaches bring more miners

Known as the "Poor Man's Gold Rush," the discovery of gold on Nome's beaches meant that anyone could work the public property without staking or recording claims. The area's population swelled to around 20,000 by 1900, and according to an article in the Nome News, the post office hired 23 clerks to handle 546,000 letters between June and August.

Veteran prospector E. C. Trelawney-Ansell later reported:

"Nome was different; it was a place where the creeks and the town itself filled with thousands of cheechakos who had never known the hardship of the trail and few if any other hardships. Worse still, the camp and surrounding country was filled with gamblers, cutthroats and murderers of the worst kind."

With more than 60 saloons, dozens of criminals, a few hundred prostitutes and dishonest officials, including an embezzling postmaster, a tax assessor who went to prison for illicit financial dealings and a federal judge who made crooked rulings, it's not surprising that robberies, murder and mayhem flourished in Nome.

Prospector turns corruption into gold

One prospector took advantage of the corruption in Nome and mined the gold-rush town's troubles.

Prospectors who'd not been successful elsewhere in Alaska dragged their outfits to Nome in the hopes that its sand would yield their fortunes.

Men sought their fortunes by panning and working long-tom sluices on the beach in Nome.

As a young man, famous American novelist Rex Beach struck out from Illinois in 1897 in search of his fortune in the gold-filled Klondike. Along with others who had some money and time, he chose to travel the all-water route.

Hopeful prospectors like Beach hopped onboard steamships leaving Seattle and other West Coast ports bound for St. Michael, where they connected with flat-bottom sternwheelers for the 1,500-plus-mile trip up the Yukon River to Dawson.

However, many travelers discovered the Yukon River boats on which they'd booked passage did not exist and found themselves stranded at St. Michael. Others jumped on boats that started up river too late in the season and got caught in the river's ice. They were forced to spend the winter in Rampart or Circle City.

Beach, who'd been studying law in Chicago when gold fever hit him, was one of those who got as far as Rampart. He eventually made his way north and spent a few years in Nome.

Writer mines Nome shenanigans

He found the once-isolated stretch of tundra fronting the beach transformed into a rip-roaring, tent and log-cabin city filled with prospectors, gamblers, claim jumpers, saloon keepers and women of ill repute.

The Nome that greeted Beach was no different than many early day gold camps. There were almost as many con men trying to separate the gold from the miners as there were miners digging for gold.

Among the rackets and racketeers was Judge Arthur H. Noyes of North Dakota, appointed to administer a newly formed judicial district created to settle the hundreds of claim disputes that plagued Nome. Noyes immediately put all contested claims into a receivership and then proceeded to exploit the claims and freeze out the miners.

It took two appeals to the 9th Circuit Court in San Francisco and two U.S. Marshals to restore order and jail Noyes and his henchmen.

Sometimes storms and ice caused problems for ships trying to get close to Nome's shores.

By July 1, 1900, Nome had become a busy frontier town with a population of around 20,000. It also boasted more than 60 saloons, dozens of criminals, a few hundred prostitutes and dishonest officials.

Beach puts pen to paper

Beach locked this and other Far North experiences into his memory bank, and after returning "Outside," put pen to paper after he heard money could be made by telling gold-rush stories.

"Back in Chicago, I was selling firebrick, lime and cement when I met a Yukon acquaintance who told me he had sold a story of one of his mining experiences for $10," Beach later recounted. "There was an empty desk where we were standing. I snagged a chair and wrote."

One of his most famous novels, "The Spoilers," tells the tale of the conniving Nome judge. The 1906 novel, which features two Yukon adventurers who duke it out over a gold claim, a beautiful saloon girl and a crooked gold commissioner, has been put to film five times – in 1914, 1923, 1930, 1942 and 1955. It helped set the public's mind about both Alaska and the Yukon.

Others mine the miners

Lured by the siren's cry of "gold," prospectors who'd not had luck elsewhere in Alaska flocked to Nome in the hopes that the sand would become their paydirt. But several adventurers, like A.F. Raynor, swarmed to the Seward Peninsula to mine the gold-mad prospectors.

Raynor, a port steward for the Blue Star Navigation Company, was working in St. Michael when he heard the news of Nome's riches. He immediately resigned his post and joined the stampede. His goal: to make "easy money" off the miners by feeding their stomachs.

Along with a stock of groceries, he purchased a large range and an assortment of crockery that had never been claimed for a hotel up the Yukon River. Raynor also bought a 30-by-40-foot tent.

The Nome stampede gave those who had yet to find their fortunes another chance. A seemingly endless stream of prospectors and freight were unloaded onto its beaches.

He piled his provisions onto the schooner *Hera* and sailed to Nome, where he was put ashore in between heavy surfs. Once he'd hauled his outfit to safety, he found the only lumber dealer and picked up enough wood, at $1 per board, to build a lunch counter and a few crude stools.

Raynor opens café

The tent city housed about 2,500 people, and every steamer arrival boosted Nome's population more. Raynor quickly set up his cook tent opposite "Tex" Rickard's saloon and gambling house, which was the largest in the camp.

He kept his menu simple, offering dishes like beans for $1 a plate; ham and eggs for $2.50; evaporated potatoes for 50 cents an order; and black coffee for 25 cents a cup. When a man with a cow walked into Raynor's café two weeks after it opened, Raynor ordered a gallon of milk to be delivered daily for $1 a quart. He then slapped up signs announcing "Fresh Milk."

But after the first order was delivered, he learned that the man had contracted to deliver 50 gallons of "fresh" milk a day to others in the community from this one remarkable cow. Raynor quickly tasted the gallon that he'd just purchased and canceled his contract. He told the "dairyman" he could make a better batch by mixing a can of evaporated milk with water.

A few days later, the man offered Raynor the beast because he couldn't get feed for it. Raynor bought the cow, skinned and dressed it, but soon learned that its steaks were too tough to eat.

"I will always believe that the cow never met her death at the hand of a butcher, but just laid down and died from malnutrition," he said later. "Such a scrawny array of bones as I had to work with I never saw before and never expect to see again."

Raynor put the carcass through a meat grinder and still made a tidy profit on hamburgers and stew.

The Poor Man's Gold Rush played itself out by the end of 1900, and after a fierce storm destroyed the business district and the beach mining operations, thousands left on boats heading south.

Many stayed behind and continued on with placer mining, but by 1910 Nome's population had dropped back to around 2,000.

A man contracted to deliver 50 gallons of "fresh" milk a day to several customers from a single cow he'd brought to Nome. This one-cow dairy didn't last long and soon was turned into hamburger and stew meat.

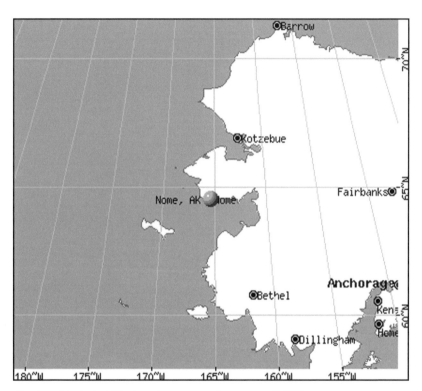

The Poor Man's Gold Rush in Nome fizzled out around 1900, so many prospectors headed toward Fairbanks to see if they could find their fortunes there.

SEA CAPTAINS, SCOUNDRELS AND NUNS

Men weren't the only prospectors seeking rich ore in Alaska's gold fields. This woman is using a rocker in a mining operation along Nome's beach.

Prospectors around Nome could bring their gold to the assay office, pictured above.

By 1902, gold bricks and other golden flakes filled Nome's Miners and Merchants Bank.

SEA CAPTAINS, SCOUNDRELS AND NUNS

27

SISTERS OF PROVIDENCE HEAD TO NOME

Many images come to mind when one thinks of gold rush days in Alaska: bearded prospectors swishing pans filled with water as they search for specks of gold; saloons beckoning the hard-working

Thousands of hopeful prospectors, like those pictured above near Nome, flooded north to find their fortunes. In 1902, the Sisters of Providence also ventured into the wilds of Alaska to build a hospital and care for the 20,000-plus miners who'd settled around Nome.

During the winter, the sisters regularly traveled Nome's rough roads by sled.

boys to forget all their troubles with a slug of whisky and a game of chance; and ladies known as "Lil" leaning against pianos, offering to help miners lighten their leather pokes.

An image that doesn't usually come to mind is that of four nuns mingling with the masses on the virtually lawless streets of Nome.

The nuns' foray into Alaska started at the-turn-of-the-last century. At the urging of two Jesuit priests named John B. Rene and Aloysius A. Jacquet, 50-year-old Sister Mary Conrad, Sister Rodrique, Sister Lambert and Sister Mary Napoleon sailed from Montreal, Canada, on June 1, 1902, bound for the shores of Alaska's Norton Sound to establish a much-needed hospital.

The influx of more than 20,000 prospectors working the gold-filled beaches of Nome brought with it a desperate need for medical facilities. Before the arrival of the Sisters of Providence, the miners relied on home remedies, often set their own broken bones and sometimes used Native healing methods.

The Sisters of Providence opened the doors to Holy Cross hospital in Nome on July 15, 1902.

After nine days of seasickness aboard the *SS Senator*, the sisters' voyage ended with a 72-hour smallpox quarantine in the Nome harbor. But once ashore, they headed toward Nome's Catholic Church, celebrated a welcoming mass with the priests and then got down to work.

Sisters open hospital

The purchase and renovation of a two-story building near the Catholic Church came to a capital debt of $7,100. But the sisters believed that Divine Providence would provide for the material needs of their mission, and they opened the doors of the Holy Cross Hospital on July 15, 1902. They convinced the city council to pick up the tab for the indigent sick at $1.50 per day, and then charged $3 to those who stayed in the wards and could pay. Patients in private rooms paid $5.

Most of the sisters' patients were miners, but they also helped other residents and Natives. A Nome News headline proclaimed, "Sisters of Providence Have Given Nome the Best Hospital in Alaska."

The nuns regularly visited the mines – on foot, horseback or dog sled – to solicit donations. They also sold tickets, as a form of insurance, for hospital care: $3 bought the miner a one-month stay, $12 for six months and $24 for one year.

The price included board, medicines, milk and liquor – as ordered by a doctor – as well as the use of bathrooms and the operating room. The miner had to pick and pay for his own doctor.

According to hospital records, a non-Catholic miner requested a baptism before his death in 1902. He then bequeathed his mining holdings to Holy Cross Hospital. The sisters quickly sold the property, which helped pay off their debt.

From left, Sisters of Providence Mary Conrad, Lambert, Mary Antoinette, Mary Napoleon and Rodrique established a hospital in Nome in 1902.

SEA CAPTAINS, SCOUNDRELS AND NUNS

Sisters of Providence outgrow hospital

During the next year, while traveling to the mines soliciting donations and selling hospital insurance, they learned about the gold that paid for many medical treatments.

"Gold abounds here and is very pure and beautiful," one sister chronicled in 1903. "Miners extract it from the bosom of the earth in the form of nuggets or dust. It is brought to the city and exchanged in the banks for minted gold and silver, and is immediately smelted and cast in bars like lead and sent out of Alaska.

"Only a small quantity is kept in Nome because of the danger that exists of being assassinated if one possesses much. In autumn, during the time of the closing of the mines and the departure of the last steamers, attempted murders are frequent."

The sisters work rapidly outgrew the original building, and by the end of 1906, the nuns had purchased land and built a larger hospital.

The Sisters of Providence turned their attention to Fairbanks, pictured above in 1909.

Sisters expand services

The community of Nome organized a carnival to help defray the costs of a new hospital in 1906 after the sisters purchased land and built a larger facility. For years thereafter, annual carnivals and bazaars helped to raise funds to run the hospital.

In 1904, Sister Mary Conrad purchased another site and built a small schoolhouse. With the addition of two new sisters who were trained in teaching, St. Joseph School opened on Oct. 5 with 25 students.

The women were proud of what they'd accomplished. They proved that they could build a hospital and a school with the help of the community, in partnership with Alaskans.

However, the survival of the sisters' hospital and school depended upon the financial health of Nome's population, which peaked in 1907-08. It then began to drop. By 1918 the mining industry had pretty much disappeared, and the Nome mission was forced to close its doors on Sept. 20 after 16 years of service.

But while the Sisters of Providence were occupied with the Holy Cross Hospital in Nome, they also were busy in Fairbanks, where they had taken over ownership of St. Joseph's Hospital in 1911.

Sisters of Providence take over hospital in Fairbanks

As they had done in Nome, the sisters organized carnivals and bazaars to help raise funds to run the Fairbanks hospital. And one of the Sisters of Providence official chronicles tells of a lucky priest who was active at St. Joseph's.

During one of the yearly carnivals, the priest bought a $1 raffle ticket for a car. He won. The priest then donated the car back to the sisters, so they got both the money from the tickets and the car.

Another year, the same priest bought the very last raffle ticket for a diamond necklace. It was a $1 ticket, as well. Again, he won! The lucky priest donated the necklace back to the sisters, too.

After Nome and Fairbanks, the Sisters of Providence turned their attention to the new railroad town in Southcentral Alaska in 1938. When they outgrew their original hospital on Eighth Avenue, they built a larger facility, pictured above in 1962, near Goose Lake in Anchorage.

The Sisters of Providence served Fairbanks until 1967, when a massive flood caused extensive damage and they permanently closed the hospital. Sister Mary Conrad turned the keys to the building over to the new administration, which renamed the facility Fairbanks Community Hospital.

Sisters begin hospital in Anchorage

In 1938, the sisters decided there was a need for medical care in Anchorage. They admitted their first patient to a 52-bed hospital, located at Eighth Avenue and L Street, on June 29, 1939. The 10,000th patient entered for health care on March 23, 1944.

Over the years, the population of Anchorage outgrew the ability of the downtown hospital. In 1958, the sisters received a 45-acre land patent and built the current hospital near Goose Lake, which is still in use today.

N A T I V E   A L A S K A N S

28

NATIVES AND THE RUSH FOR GOLD

A Dawson newspaper printed an editorial in 1900 that voiced concern over the treatment of Alaska's indiginous peoples. The points made by the editor of The Klondike Nugget were not resolved for decades.

"It will doubtless happen with these Indians as it has happened with every other aboriginal race that has come in contact with what we are pleased to term civilization. Civilization will ultimately wipe the Indians out of existence. This is the whole story in a nutshell, and it is apparent that the Indians themselves have a very well-defined notion that such will prove to be the case. They see the land, which they considered their own, taken away from them without even their permission being asked. The game, upon which they have been accustomed to depend very largely for subsistence, is being driven back into the mountains, and when the game has all disappeared the Indians see nothing ahead for them but extinction.

"Formerly the Indians owned all the ground, all the fish and all the game. Now they own nothing. Then they could do as they pleased, with no one to interfere with them. Now they are liable to arrest for any breach of the law, just as a white man.

"How they could lose all they once possessed and get nothing in return is something they cannot comprehend. The case is worth consideration from the authorities. Whether or not the Indians possess any legal rights in the premises, there are certain moral obliga-

Above: Five Chilkat men with heavy packs rest while a stampeder adjusts the load atop one of two oxen along the Chilkoot Pass Trail.

Upper right: Metlakatla Indians pole a canoe up the Dyea River. Photographer Frank LaRoche noted: "They have in transit a knock-down boat, the bow of which is a conspicuous feature. They receive $200 for taking two such boats from the head of canoe navigation to the summit of Chilkoot Pass, about 10 miles. Canoes can be readily obtained from the Indians, but it is not advisable to attempt to use them without the assistance of Indians who are familiar with the frail birch-bark vessels. Like many other things, they are easily maneuvered when properly understood. These canoes can be secured to carry considerable weights."

Lower right: Chilkat Indians, such as the Native women guiding the boat in this picture, earned money by freighting Klondikers' supplies up the Dyea River. These boats are regular dugouts, made from large timber and drawing about 8 inches of water, yet they carry 1,000 pounds or more of freight. The trading companies never paid the Natives in cash until the summer of 1897. That's when the Indians, learning that deckhands on steamers made $1 an hour, went on strike and refused to work for less than $2 per hour. When the trading companies finally gave in and agreed to pay that amount, the Natives continued to strike until they received $5.

Above: Native Alaskans dried fish on racks outside Nome and often helped feed hungry prospectors who were unprepared for winter in the North County.

Below: Native women in Nome use metal buckets to collect berries.

tions involved which should not be overlooked. If there is any danger of actual want among them, the matter should be promptly looked into and relief granted."
– Editorial in The Klondike Nugget on April 1, 1900

At the time of the U.S. purchase of Alaska, most Native Alaskans lived the traditional lifestyles of their ancestors, hunting and fishing for a living and governing themselves through ancient tribal systems.

But the influx of white traders, prospectors and settlers into the territory after the purchase changed their way of life forever.

For some, whites brought illness, alcohol, destruction of hunting grounds and forests and disregard of traditional lifestyles.

European trade goods, including tea kettles and buckets, may have helped ease the burden of daily life for the Native people.

But while some whites mistreated the Native population because they considered them racially and culturally inferior, others, like George Washington Carmack who loved the Natives, treated them with respect and relied upon their knowledge of the land to survive.

Native peoples trapped, hunted and fished for the miners who trickled into the territory. They also provided transportation for men, messages and supplies, and they saved many lives by helping those who were ill-prepared for Alaska's elements.

Along the Yukon River, Alaska Commercial Company traders like Leroy "Jack" McQuesten, Arthur Harper and Al Mayo amicably traded goods for furs with the local tribes and introduced them to a new way of life.

Lt. Frederick Schwatka, a U.S. cavalry officer who floated the Yukon River in 1883, described a trading scene he observed between McQuestern and a Native trapper, which went on for hours, by saying the endless bargaining "would have put Job in a frenzy."

During this period of time, fur was the currency of choice. U.S. Army Corps of Engineers Capt. Charles W. Raymond noted the prices of various pelts in 1869 during his journey up the Yukon River:

"The beaver skin was the standard unit of measurement. A gun was sold to an Indian for 18 beaver skins. Marten were traded at the rate of two marten to a beaver and other skins were set at lower values. All trading was done by barter, and in addition to guns, the Hudson's Bay Company traded pocketknives, pants, shirts, cloth, bullets, knives, pots, buttons, thread, handkerchiefs, 'Paris neckties' and 'English belts.'"

As word of gold found along tributaries of the Yukon spread, the Chilkoot Indians in Southeast Alaska reaped some benefits by charging a fee to pack the white men's outfits across a route through the mountains that they had monopolized for years.

For centuries Natives traveled through different mountain passes, including the Chilkoot Pass, to trade. The Chilkoots tenaciously guarded their pass and thus controlled access to the Interior, which resulted in a trade monopoly with other Native peoples of Alaska and the Yukon.

Klondikers and Indian packers take a break as they climb the Chilkoot Pass Trail.

The Southern Tutchone had many items to interest Chilkat traders, including furs and un-tanned skins of moose, caribou and sheep, as well as lynx, marten and beaver. The Tutchone also had raw copper, sinew and yellow lichen that the Chilkats used to dye their blankets.

The Chilkats provided edible seaweed, cedar baskets, dentalium shell ornaments, slaves, grease from eulachon – a small oil-rich fish – and European trade goods.

European trade goods, which included blankets, calico, kettles, axes, knives, coffee, flour and tobacco, helped to ease the burden of daily life for Native people. They also altered traditional trade patterns, as the Tutchone traded surplus European goods with neighbors farther into the Interior.

The Chilkoot Indians' domination of the costal mountain route proved to be beneficial for them as white prospectors headed into the territory and Alaska marched toward a cash economy.

A sturdy people, the men could pack up to 200 pounds on their backs and women and children could carry about 75 pounds each.

"… they always exacted what the traffic would bear, so that by the time of the Klondike stampede the price had reached a dollar a pound. Thus, without ever sinking a pan into the creek beds of the Yukon, the canny Chilkoots became rich men," according to Pierre Berton in "The Klondike Fever."

Before contact with the whites, the Natives had little or no use for gold. But once they learned its value, and the value of coins, many tried to hoard the precious metals. New York journalist Tappan Adney, who was sent to the Yukon in 1897 to chronicle the stampede to the gold fields around Dawson, wrote:

"They are taking all the small change out of circulation. They come to the traders several times a day, making a trifling purchase to get change, then store it away. The small change problem is indeed a serious one. There is not enough small currency to do business with. The gamblers and the Indians are getting it all."

The traditional Native way of life also was changed by the arrival of well-intentioned missionaries who wanted to keep the Natives from drinking, gambling and carousing with non-Native miners. Many missionaries discouraged Natives from speaking their languages and changed their methods of worship. The Indian societies had highly developed spiritual beliefs that weren't recognized or respected by Christian missionaries.

Most Natives lived far from the mining camps, but some were lured to the camps by prospects of social and economic opportunities. This family in Nome has set up their skin tent next to prospectors' canvas tents on the beach in Nome around 1900.

NATIVE ALASKANS

This crew of Natives hired on to cut and load cordwood fuel for the steamers of the Alaska Commercial Company. Native laborers were paid about two-thirds of what white workers were paid for the same work.

Tlingit chief Kah-du-shan summed up the feelings of many of his tribesmen when he spoke openly in Juneau about the missionaries and whites coming into the territory:

"The missionaries and teachers tell us that no one but God make the people. We know that the same God made us. And the God placed us here. White people are smart; our people are not as smart as white people. Just like the sun shining on this earth. They are powerful. They have the power. They have men of wars. It is not right for such powerful people as you are to take away from poor people like we are, our creeks and hunting grounds."

While most Natives lived far away from the mining camps, some were lured to the camps by prospects of social and economic opportunities and learned how to survive in a wage-based and in-kind environment. In spite of racist overtones, Natives served as guides, packers and laborers doing odd jobs such as cutting cordwood for

Above: Some Native women made and sold mitts, hats, mukluks and other clothing to stampeders.

Upper right: After the Treadwell Mines opened near Juneau in 1881, women came from nearby villages to sell baskets, beaded clothing and other wares to the gold miners and tourists.

Lower right: A Chilkat Indian posed as a packer in the studio of Eric A. Hegg during the Klondike Gold Rush.

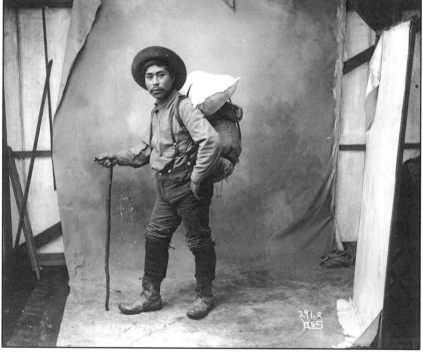

the many riverboats. White laborers made between $6 and $10 a day, Native workers only made between $4 and $8 for the same job.

Native women reaped some benefits of the new cash economy, as well, as they made and sold mitts, hats, mukluks and other clothing to the stampeders. They also sold meat and fish that they hunted and caught.

Many Native women also became wives of miners and traders. Ivan Pavloff, a Creole trader stationed at Nulato, married a local woman, Malanka. Their children all figured prominently in the development of gold mining on the Yukon River. One of their daughters, Erinia Pavloff Cherosky Callahan, worked with her husband as a translator for the traders. Their other daughter, Kate Pavloff Sonnickson, married one of the early prospectors and eventually moved to California. Their son, John Minook, discovered gold at Rampart, while son Pitka Pavloff and son-in-law Sergei Cherosky discovered gold at Birch Creek, leading to the development of Circle City.

Another part Russian, part Native woman known as "Reindeer Mary" or "Sinrock Mary" eased her way from a subsistence way of life and barter system into the world of commerce by selling reindeer meat to the never-ending stream of stampeders coming into the Nome area in the early 1900s to become the richest Native woman of the time.

29

RICHEST NATIVE WOMAN IN THE NORTH

While the various gold rushes to Alaska did not overwhelmingly benefit most Natives, one baby girl born in 1865 would become the richest Native woman in the North and grow famous because

Mary Makrikoff, later known as Sinrock Mary, found Nome, shown here circa 1900, much different than her home village of St. Michael.

of reindeer. Born to an Inupiat Eskimo mother and a Russian trader father, Mary Makrikoff was raised in St. Michael on the southern shore of Alaska's Norton Sound. Her mother called her "Changunak."

Mary grew up speaking fluent Russian, English and Inupiaq. Her skills with these languages made her a valuable resource for ship captains and government officials who traveled to her village. She also learned skin tanning and sewing, how to preserve edible plants and how to share in the Eskimo way from her mother.

Sinrock Mary in 1906.

In 1889 she met and married Inupiat Charlie Antisarlook, and the couple moved to Cape Nome. Mary found her new home quite different from the relatively cosmopolitan coastal village of St. Michael, a trading post on the Bering Sea that saw foreign ships dock almost daily.

"There were no people there (in Nome)," she said later in life. "Not any groceries, either. Their food wasn't like what the Eskimos of St. Michael work hard to have."

Her new life in Nome meant she had to learn how to live on "real simple food, like whale meat, seal oil, rabbits and ptarmigan." But the determined young woman did learn the subsistence ways and her family thrived.

Mary and Charlie lived in a settlement outside of Nome called Sinrock, where they helped the U.S. government with its reindeer herds for several years. Then the government gave the couple 500 animals, thus making them the first Natives to be given their own herd.

However, disaster struck when Charlie died during a measles epidemic in 1900. After his death, Mary had to fight hard to keep her reindeer. Because she was a Native woman, her brothers-in-law asserted that she couldn't own property.

But after a lengthy legal battle, she won the right to keep half the herd and became known as Sinrock Mary. She often could be seen, a solitary Eskimo woman, driving her herd across the tundra.

When news of gold sparkling on Nome's beaches brought 20,000 hungry stampeders to the small village, Mary seized the opportunity to supply them with fresh meat. Since all the miners' supplies came by boat from "Outside," high prices were the order of the day for any kind of fresh food. Sinrock Mary made a tidy sum selling her reindeer meat to the miners, the U.S. Army station and stores.

Sinrock Mary helped the U.S. government care for a reindeer herd brought to Nome in the early 1900s from Lapland.

While her successful reindeer meat business made her the richest Native woman in the North in no time, her fortune came at a high price. She constantly had to dodge gold-rush prospectors who followed her across the tundra.

These men were desperate to get her reindeer to use as food, as well as to haul supplies and equipment to their claims. But Mary would not hand over her reindeer. She had worked too hard to lose her herd to any man.

When she refused to give them the animals, the men called her names and shot at the reindeer to scatter the herd. But Mary, a large, imposing woman with dark curly hair and a traditional Inupiat tattoo on her chin, didn't budge.

So the miners changed their tactics. When they found intimidation wouldn't work, they tried to court Mary, offering her money, liquor and even marriage so they could gain control of her herd.

Mary successfully fought off the prospectors' advances, but the constant pestering finally got to her.

Fed up with the miners' threats and uninvited attentions, Mary left Nome in 1901 and moved her herd to Unalakleet. The following year, she married Andrew Andrewuk, an Inupiat who had no real interest in her reindeer. Mary tended her herd for many years, and eventually grew it to more than 1,500 animals.

While she was successful multiplying her reindeer herd, Mary never had any offspring of her own. However, she did adopt 11 children. She taught them, as well as Inupiat men, to care for reindeer, and many of her children grew up to have herds of their own.

When "Reindeer Mary" died in 1948, she left a legacy of compassion and generosity. People still tell stories about how she shared her wealth in the Eskimo way.

SETTLEMENTS SPRING UP

30

BIRTH OF FORT YUKON

Canadian voyagers, English and Russian fur trappers, and gold seekers of all nations sought their fortunes in the Yukon Valley. The villages they established — Fort Yukon, the first English-speaking settlement along the great river; Circle City, once the "world's largest log cabin city;" Rampart, a picturesque gold rush camp and locale of one of Rex Beach's novels — still cling to life and are reminders of Alaska's picturesque past.

Circle City's fire department, pictured here in 1901, was rudimentary at best.

In that past, great sternwheelers proudly carried passengers and freight back and forth between Whitehorse and St. Michael. The wood-burning engines are stilled; the vessels lie rotting along the riverbank. Instead of riding river boats and dog sleds, one can travel in comfort now on the "magic carpet" of air travel. Instead of weeks or months to reach a destination, now it only takes minutes or hours. But it is easy to imagine what it was like back in pioneer times when one arrives at the villages.

Fort Yukon, which can be reached by air from Fairbanks, was described by famous columnist Ernie Pyle as being "a half mile from the ends of the earth." Its story is a page out of Alaska's history as its trading post proudly boasts:

"We sell everything from Tractors to Thimbles, including Furs, Finery, Fish and Flowers!"

The village store is a direct descendent of the Hudson's Bay Post first established more than 100 years ago. John Bell, an employee of the Hudson's Bay Company, reached the Yukon by way of the Porcupine River in 1846. A year later, Alexander Murray, another Hudson's Bay man, started a new post about three miles upstream from the mouth of the Porcupine, well beyond the Arctic Circle. Although the Hudson's Bay traders heard stories of gold along the Yukon, they paid them no heed because they were interested only in the rich fur trade.

This was the most far-flung of their great chain of posts that stretched across the continent, and so isolated that when the com-

The arms displayed on the Hudson's Bay Company seal were assumed by the company as early as 1678. The cross is red or gold, sometimes green. On either side of the shield is an elk, and under the shield is the famous motto: "Pro Pelle Cutem" – For the pelts that we collect, we risk our skins.

mander shipped a cargo of furs to London, reports were not received until seven years later.

In order to withstand Russian attack, Murray built the fort especially strong. As he wrote in his journal:

"We live on good terms with the Natives and fear nothing except to see two boatloads of Russians heave around the point."

The Hudson's Bay people held down their lonely outpost for 22 years. They were finally forced to move out, not by the Russians, but by the Americans.

When the Americans, under the command of Capt. Charles Raymond of the U.S. Army, jumped ashore from the first steamboat to ascend the Yukon that far, they were met by all of Fort Yukon's inhabitants and treated with great hospitality.

On Aug. 9, 1869, the Union Jack came down and the Stars and Stripes were hoisted over the first English-speaking settlement on the river. The Alaska Commercial Company assumed operations at the trading post and the Canadians withdrew peaceably up the Porcupine River to a spot they thought was in Canada. However, they had to make two more moves before they finally got out of America.

Native Alaskans within the Yukon Flats at the time of European contact included several bands of Athabascan Indians, who were higly mobile hunters and excellent trappers.

The original post is gone – engulfed by the voracious Yukon River that is constantly gnawing away at the river's banks. However, the Northern Commercial store was its direct descendant. Fur remained a medium of exchange, just as it was in the Hudson's Bay days, for Fort Yukon always has been considered the "fur mother lode" of the North.

Trappers from outlying settle-

Fort Yukon Indians greeted the Schieffelin brothers during their prospecting trip to the area in 1882-1883.

ments on the Porcupine, Chandalar, Big and Little Black and the Christian rivers brought their furs to the outpost. And although the decline in fur prices cut down on trappers' income, strings of glossy pelts still hung cheek by jowl with modern conveniences in "The Store."

Like its progenitor, the American store had an interesting and intriguing inventory. Along with the electric washing machines, it sold pounds of rickrack braid, colored yarn and Czechoslovakian beads of all colors. The Athabascan craftsmen, famous for their hand-sewn bead artistry, worked with delicate pastel colors and original designs, not on the usual loom, but by hand. They traded their hand-work for food and clothing at the store, and in an area poor from low fur prices, this often meant the difference between being hungry and cold and having enough to eat and wear when the temperature dipped to 60 degrees below zero.

Along with Hudson's Bay traders came missionaries from the Church of England, who established the oldest missionary station on

Rampart became a boomtown after John Minook, a half-Russian and half-Native prospector, dug 15 feet down an 8-foot-square hole and discovered large quantities of gold.

the Yukon River. When Capt. Raymond and the Americans arrived in 1869, they found the Rev. William Carpenter Bompas, later Bishop Bompas of the Yukon, in residence.

After the Americans "took over" Fort Yukon, the Episcopal Church continued its missionary work started by the Church of England, and in 1904, Archdeacon Hudson Stuck arrived at Fort Yukon. Besides his missionary work and the authorship of several very readable books, Stuck is remembered as the leader of the first party to reach the South Peak of Mount McKinley, North America's highest mountain.

Gold was discovered on Birch Creek in 1893, and the community of Circle rapidly expanded to a population of more than 1,000 people during the boom that followed. And although the gold-rush era ended, fur trapping contined to expand, and by the 1920s Fort Yukon had become the most important fur center in Alaska.

When Stuck died in 1920, his expressed wish to be buried in Fort Yukon was respected and his grave is shown to visitors with pride. The villagers whisper that they see his spirit wandering through the ruins of the hospital he established in 1915. It was torn down in 1956, and the orphanage he also established was turned into a day clinic.

During those early days, moss-covered roofed log cabins and fish wheels dotted the river bank at Fort Yukon, and if every river has its voice, the voice of the Yukon might well have been, as Paul Brooks said, "the rhythmic groan and splash of the fish wheels as the giant wheels turn slowly in the current, their webbed baskets now and then scraping up a silvery fish from the thousands pouring upstream."

Two hundred and thirty miles downstream from Fort Yukon is the almost deserted village of Rampart, once an important trading post and supply center for thousands of miners on Minook and Hess creeks.

While George Washington Carmack and his friends were busy on Bonanza Creek in 1896, a half-Russian and half-Native prospector named John Minook was searching for gold about 700 miles down river from Dawson at the mouth of Minook Creek.

"Were it not for the Klondike, Minook would itself have caused a stampede from the United States," said Pierre Berton in his book, "The Klondike Fever."

By 1897, the village of Rampart swelled to 1,000, including the famous writer Rex Beach, who landed in town with a fur-lined sleeping bag, a rifle, a dogskin suit and a mandolin. Dilapidated cabins brought $800 and lots fetched up to $1,200.

Now, when one walks up and down its deserted paths, it's difficult to imagine the busy scenes of the 1890s when eager gold-seekers jumped ashore from busy riverboats and crowded into the stores open day and night, or into the saloons alive with men entering and leaving through their swinging doors.

But other gold-rush towns, like Fairbanks, had staying power.

31

FAIRBANKS STARTED FROM RICH BANKS

Felix Pedro joined the Klondike rush in 1898 from the Carbonado coal mines in Washington state. But his lucky number failed to come up, so he and Frank Costa, another Italian prospector, wandered over into the valley of the Tanana to prospect its streams and creeks. Deviled by mosquitoes and forced at times to eat some of their dogs, they traveled through the wooded valleys, climbed the rugged hills and faced moose and grizzly bears. In July 1902, Pedro struck gold on a small stream just 24 miles from the spot on the Chena River that later became Fairbanks.

While Pedro was poking around searching for gold, a trader was beating his way up the Tanana on the riverboat *Lavelle Young*. Capt. E.T. Barnette wanted to establish a trading post on the upper river at Tanacross. By chance, he got into the Chena, a tributary of the Tanana. It was a lucky accident for him, as his trading post got in on the ground floor of the new strike.

A horde of prospectors rushed in to the diggings during the autumn of 1902, and by summer 1904, the news had spread to Canada and stampeders were hurrying from the Yukon River down the Tanana in scows, rafts, steamers and small boats.

When they reached their destination, they found a few log cabins clustered around several large, corrugated iron warehouses – and a scene of utter confusion. Household goods, barrels of whiskey, kegs of

After Felix Pedro discovered gold in the Interior in 1902, hordes of prospectors rushed into the area and built Fairbanks along the Chena River.

beer, lumber, steam-thaw boilers and crates of food were all jumbled together in chaotic disorder in a small clearing of spruce trees.

Soon the smell of freshly cut lumber was everywhere. Saws whined and the sound of hammers rat-a-tat-tatted day and night as cabins, hotels, stores and saloons hastily went up among the stumps and chaos.

Tall brass scales took the place of cash registers and gold dust the place of money. Miners tossed their pokes over the counter to the bartender to weigh out enough dust to pay the bill – $16 an ounce in trade was the current rate.

Many establishments offered to supply liquid refreshment and entertainment, including the Northern, the Tanana, the Senate and Washington saloons, the Pioneer, the Minook and the Flora Dora Music Hall.

The Fairbanks Hotel not only offered a restaurant and saloon with "Monte Carlo games on the square," it also hosted a family concert every evening. And "I'm sport enough to give the preachers a square deal," said the proprietor when he heard that an Episcopal missionary and a Presbyterian preacher were looking for a place to hold services. He offered his saloon and politely covered the glasses and decanters with his only white sheet.

Some of the prospectors in the new gold fields struck paydirt. Dan McCarty found gold on what later was named Fairbanks Creek. J.A. Mathieson located more on Little Eldorado, D.A. Shea found rich prospects on Dome Creek and T.M. Gilmore struck it rich on Vault Creek. Gold shipments rose from $35,000 in 1903 to $3,750,000 in 1905.

While Fairbanks became a seething, exciting and feverish center of trade, one churchgoing highwayman couldn't resist the temptation to steal from gold-toting miners.

32

BLUE PARKA BANDIT

The "Blue Parka Bandit" had struck again. People chuckled over his latest exploit, although usually his holdups were no laughing matter. This time, however, Alaskans felt they had a good joke on Bishop Peter Trimble Rowe, a popular Episcopalian missionary who was in the last party robbed by the daring highwayman.

Peter Trimble Rowe, Bishop of Alaska, was robbed by the Blue Parka Bandit.

As always, the bandit's mask and blue parka hid his face. He pointed a Winchester at his victims.

"Line up, put your pokes and valuables on the trail and mush on," he ordered.

Bishop Rowe had no poke of gold, but he placed his little wad of money on the heap with the rest. Then he couldn't resist chiding the bandit.

"Friend," he asked in his gentle voice. "Is this the way you treat a minister of the gospel?"

Prospectors along the gold-producing creeks around Fairbanks had to watch out for the Blue Parka Bandit.

"Are you a minister?" asked the man in the blue parka.

"I am Bishop Rowe of the Episcopal Church."

"Oh," said the highwayman in surprise. "Well, I'm pleased to meet you, Bishop. Of course I won't rob you. Take your money back and take that poke with the shoestring on it, too. Why, damn it all, Bishop, I'm a member of your church!"

Although people were amused at this incident, the plunderings of the bold bandit in blue generally evoked curses from miners scattered along the gold-producing creeks near Fairbanks in the early 1900s. No longer did they dare travel singly or even in groups with their gold.

They finally organized a posse to make the rounds of Cleary, Pedro, Dome, Little Eldorado, Vault, Fox, Ester and all the rest of the streams. The posse picked up the gold, and escorted by a half-dozen armed and mounted men, the little processions traveled toward

Fairbanks with a man behind, a man ahead and four men guarding the gold.

By 1905, all manner of men had crowded into Fairbanks, Alaska's newest mining camp, and the outlying creeks to get their share of the gold that a 42-year-old immigrant Italian miner had first found in the vicinity three years before.

Down the Yukon and the 300 miles of the Tanana sailed the motley flotilla. Across from the Koyukuk and Rampart regions rushed more stampeders. Up from St. Michael came the unfortunate ones who hadn't struck it rich in Nome. They streamed in from Valdez and the Copper River Valley. Trails converged on the new gold camp from every direction.

The man in the blue parka made sure he got his share of the gold diggings, too, even though he didn't wield a pick or shovel. But his

Fed up with numerous robberies, prospectors in the Interior finally organized an armed posse to pick up loads of gold for transport to Fairbanks.

SETTLEMENTS SPRING UP

robbing days came to an end when people noticed that a man named Hendrickson, a fugitive from prison, always seemed to be in the vicinity of the holdups. When various circumstances connected him with the robberies, he was captured and jailed. And evidence disclosed that he constantly visited (when his "work" permitted) the Episcopal Church library where he was known as a reader of good books.

Authorities may have captured the Blue Parka Bandit, but the citizens of Fairbanks weren't to hear the last of him for a while. Since the federal judge was out of the country, the bandit's trial had to wait and the long winter in jail proved too monotonous for Hendrickson and another inmate, a horse thief named Thornton.

Somehow the pair acquired a knife. When their guard opened the cell door to bring them food one day, the men knocked him down and then stabbed him, crippling him for life.

Lawmen captured the miscreants again, and when the judge returned in late summer, the inmates each received a 15-year sus-

The Blue Parka Bandit was sentenced to do time in McNeil Island Prison in Washington state, pictured here in 1909.

The *Lavelle Young*, pictured above stored for winter, steamed out of Fairbanks in 1905 with the Blue Parka Bandit onboard.

pended sentence for breaking jail and stabbing the guard. The judge then sentenced them to serve time for their other misdeeds in a federal prison in Washington state.

Convicts finally leave town

When the citizens of Fairbanks saw the convicts board the *Lavelle Young* under the watchful eye of a federal marshal, they breathed a collective sigh of relief that the two wouldn't be in their town jail another winter.

The *Lavelle Young* was one of the last boats going out that season and was crowded to the gunwales with miners, prospectors, gamblers, confidence men, capitalists, merchants, musicians, theatrical and vaudeville performers, respectable women and some not so respectable. Also onboard were about 20 miners with their dogs, canoes and provisions, bound for a new strike reported up one of the Yukon tributaries. The crowded discomfort was disregarded, for everyone was anxious to get out before freeze up. For a while, it looked doubtful that they would. Whether the Blue Parka Bandit was the jinx can't be stated positively, but bad luck dogged the *Lavelle Young* on this journey.

First off, a piece of machinery broke and repairs took a whole day. Then, after steaming for only a few hours, it failed once more and a cylinder head blew into the river.

There was nothing to do but tie up to a small island where ice floating by warned that winter and freeze up were close at hand. With limited provisions, and the nearest telegraph station 150 miles away, passengers worried about their fate. Fortunately, a boat coming up the river agreed to take a message to the telegraph station, and shortly the owners of the *Lavelle Young* learned of their boat's predicament and sent another of their ships to help out. On Oct. 3, the *Seattle No. 3* arrived to connect her cables to the stricken ship and propel her up the river.

The passengers remained good-humored. Concerts and vaudeville entertainments by trained talent took place every evening. Card-playing and gambling occupied much of the spare time. And there was always conversation. One of the most interesting topics among this diverse assemblage was the presence of the Blue Parka Bandit onboard their boat. Before long, everyone knew that he was in a center stateroom that opened off the dining hall.

"Thornton is in there, too, and a couple of more prisoners – a forger and the fellow who got away with gold from the Express Company," they gossiped.

The stateroom that held the four prisoners was a double one with three berths on each side, one above the other. The door's handle had been taken off and the marshal kept the only key on his person. The one window was barred and guarded night and day. The marshal himself always attended to the prisoners' meals, and spoons were their only eating utensils.

"They surely don't take any chances with those fellows," the passengers commented, as they watched the precautions with interest. "There's always a guard in front of the door and one pacing back and forth before that barred window. Guess the Blue Parka Man won't get away this time!"

A 30-pound weight clamped onto prisoners' boots stopped many convicts from escaping during the early days of law enforcement. This "Oregon Boot" is on display at the State Troopers' Museum in downtown Anchorage.

The marshal was certainly doing his best. Both Hendrickson and Thornton had "Oregon Boots" attached to their shoes – circular disks of iron, weighing 30 pounds and clamped around the men's ankles by means of an inside hinge. These were secured by bolts sunk in small sockets, locked by screwing them tightly with a key. Iron bars with the ends bent upward were screwed to the soles of their shoes, and the upturned ends attached to the boots in such a manner that they were held off the ankles. This didn't make for easy walking and the prisoners got little exercise. As the trip wore on, Hendrickson and Thornton grew weak and pale from their close confinement, and some of the passengers even expressed sympathy for them.

"Why can't you give them some relief from those cramped quarters and take off the boots for a while? They can't get away," they said.

The marshal, however, remained adamant.

"These are desperate men," he answered patiently. "They've broken jail before, and they aren't going to get away while I'm guarding them."

Brave words, but spoken too soon.

Bandit escapes

The dinner gong sounded at 5:30 p.m. on Oct. 6 while the *Lavelle Young* and *Seattle No. 3* were tied up at the Nation City wood yard to take on fuel. Passengers gathered around the tables with good appetites. As they started their main course, the outside guard burst in. He hurried over to the marshal, whispered something to him, and then ran out. The marshal jumped up, pulled out his revolver and rushed to the door of the prisoners' stateroom. He then quickly inserted a key into the lock. Pointing his gun ahead of him, the marshal pushed open the door. The inside guard backed him up, also with drawn revolver.

"They've escaped!" someone shouted.

Passengers onboard the *Lavelle Young* had just been seated for dinner when a guard burst into the dining room, similar to that pictured here, and announced that the Blue Parka Bandit had escaped.

Panic ensued instantly. Women screamed, and a few fainted. A confused rush in all directions followed, with some of the passengers hiding under tables, others running to lock themselves in their staterooms, and some rushing out on deck.

The marshal found only two prisoners left in the stateroom. The Blue Parka Bandit and his horse thief sidekick had escaped. The marshal and guards frantically searched both vessels, going through all the staterooms and inspecting every corner above and below decks. But they found no trace of the daring escapees.

Both steamers immediately focused their searchlights up and down the riverbank against the thick, dark woods bordering it. The boats stayed docked until midnight while a search went on for the fugitives, to no avail.

Everyone knew the desperate characters of Hendrickson and Thronton, and one of the men from Nation City took off over the trail to warn the miners on the creek. An Indian, who happened to be at the community, jumped into his canoe and started downriver to warn a camp of his tribesmen, 50 miles below.

"It's going to be a hard job finding them," one of the miners remarked. "Hendrickson used to work a claim around here, so he knows the country. It won't be any cinch to catch up with that bird."

And so it proved. Finally, the marshal had to let the boats proceed, and about midnight they started up the river again. A reward was left with an old Montana ex-sheriff occupying one of the cabins at Nation City for the capture of the fugitives dead or alive, and the marshal hoped to get further instructions from Fairbanks when he got to Eagle and could send a wire.

While the searchlights had been probing the darkness along the riverbank, Hendrickson and Thornton were hiding in the thick woods nearby. Their getaway hadn't been too difficult. The escape artist, Hendrickson, engineered it. Somehow, he'd obtained a broken piece of jeweler's file before leaving Fairbanks. Inserting the file into his pipe, he then had smoked a crust around it so that when the pipe was examined, no one noticed the presence of the file.

In the stateroom, Hendrickson found that two small hooks had been left screwed into the wall of the room. The curtain that had hung on a thin brass tube about two feet long had been taken away, but the brass tube and hooks had been left. The rod, the hooks and his jeweler's file were all that Hendrickson needed.

A most ingenious mechanic, he filed off about eight inches of the brass tube and divided it into two pieces. One was flattened out and filed into a small saw. The other piece was used as a key to unscrew the bolts locking the Oregon Boots. The ceiling of the stateroom presented no problem. It was only a half-inch thick and constituted the roof of the steamboat. Forward of this room was a ladder descending to the lower deck.

With the hooks, Hendrickson made adjoining holes through the roof, and lying on their backs in the upper berth, he and Thornton took turns sawing, while the other two stood close to the window to obscure the guard's view. After each period of work, the holes and saw incisions were carefully filled with soap, the white substance completely obliterating the evidence. Finally, a section exactly 15 inches long and 10 inches wide was cut out of the ceiling, but left in

The Blue Parka Bandit ecaped from the *Lavelle Young* as it sat waiting for fuel at the wood yard in Nation City, pictured above.

place until the right opportunity arrived.

The opportunity came when the boat stopped at Nation City. Taking out the screws that attached the iron bars to their shoes, the outlaws were ready. While the dinner gong rang loudly, Hendrickson ripped out the ceiling. The other prisoners backed up against the window. Then he and Thornton climbed up through the hole, and Hendrickson led the way as they descended the ladder and crossed over the other boat to shore.

The Blue Parka Bandit was sentenced to do time in the McNeil Island Prison, pictured above.

One mishap occurred. As Thornton descended the ladder and stepped out on deck, he met the outside guard who looked at him, but without recognition. On shore, the prisoners immediately ran into the woods, stumbling in the darkness.

Back on the boat, the outside guard who had run into Thornton, did a double take. Coming face to face so suddenly with him, he hadn't credited his vision and continued to pace back and forth a few times before he realized what he had seen. Then he ran to the window, saw that two of the prisoners were missing, and rushed inside to tell the marshal that Hendrickson and Thornton had escaped.

Convicts hide out

And hidden by brush, the two fugitives shuddered and shivered in the northern wilderness, with winter approaching and the temperature close to zero. In a weak physical condition already, their lot was indeed desperate, for they had no warm clothing, matches or food.

"God, it's cold," Thornton muttered. "And I sure wish we could have waited until after dinner to escape."

"Eat some frozen blueberries," Hendrickson unsympathetically replied. "You wanted to come along, so quit bellyaching. This is better than dragging around that Oregon Boot, isn't it? I tell you, I know this country. We'll find a cabin, get in out of the cold and pick up some grub and warm clothes."

Nation Creek is about 100 miles below Eagle, which is on the boundary between Canada and Alaska. Three miles above its mouth sat Nation City, with three or four cabins and the wood camp where steamers "wooded up." Twelve miles above Nation City was a roadhouse and scattered up and down Nation Creek about a dozen cabins, some occupied by miners who intended to work their claims all winter.

The fugitives first tried to find an empty cabin near the wood yard. They crept silently to the settlement, but men milling around talking about the escape and reward thwarted their plan.

Since they had no chance to break into a cabin there, the two escapees turned away to find something more available. Off they struck across country for the roadhouse Hendrickson knew about. He had to keep urging his companion on, because Thornton had come close to the end of his endurance.

The men finally reached their destination and found the occupants afraid to keep the desperate men out. They ate and then took turns sleeping. Early the next morning, they began trekking downriver. But Thornton didn't make it very far.

"It's no use – I'm done up," he told his companion as he sagged to the ground.

"Stay here, then," commanded Hendrickson. "I'll get hold of a boat somehow. That'll make travel easier."

Hendrickson hadn't gone far when it looked like his luck had turned. Over the sand bar he saw a man coming toward him towing a canoe. At once Hendrickson ran into the woods bordering the stream and found a heavy club. He watched as the man came near and then jumped out with the upraised weapon.

"I need that boat," he said. "If you don't row me, I'll kill you and if you don't row where I tell you, I'll upset the canoe."

The fugitive compelled the man to get into the stern while he pushed the boat out to deeper water. But he hadn't noticed a gun in the bottom of the boat, and when he leaped into the canoe, he found himself looking into the gun's barrel.

"All right, Hendrickson," said the gun's owner, the ex-sheriff from Montana. "Start rowing."

In the meantime, Thornton had seen the marshal approaching up the river and had gone back to the roadhouse to give himself up. He'd had enough of freedom in the wilderness and considered the price of liberty too high to pay.

The marshal had received telegraphed instructions from Fairbanks to go back to Nation Creek and retake the fugitives. He lost no time and escorted them to the federal prison in Washington.

But Hendrickson wasn't through. He had one more escape to his credit. After his recapture from the Washington prison, authorities moved him to the government prison at Leavenworth, Kan. There he remained until his discharge on Feb. 11, 1920.

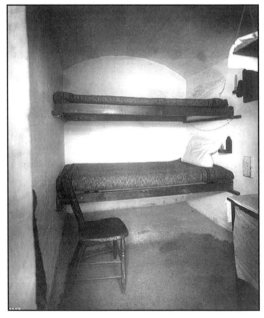

The Blue Parka Bandit managed to escape from his cell, similar to the one pictured to the right, after he was finally delivered to McNeil Island Prison in Washington state. Authorities transfered him to the government prison at Leavenworth, Kan.

BIBLIOGRAPHY

Adney, Tappan. *The Klondike Stampede*. New York, NY: 1900.

Alexan, Nickafor. Recorded and transcribed history of Tyonek.

Alexander, Hartley. *The Mythology of All Races*. New York, NY: 1964.

Allan, A.A. *Gold, Men and Dogs*. New York, NY: 1931.

Allen, Lt. Henry T. *Report of an Expedition to the Copper, Tanana and Koyukuk Rivers in the Territory of Alaska in the Year 1885*.

Ameigh, George C. Jr. and Yule M. Chaffin, *Alaska's Kodiak Island*. Author: 1962.

Andrews, Clarence L. *The Story of Alaska*. Caldwell, ID: Caxton Printers Ltd., 1947.

Archer, S.A. *A Heroine of the North*.

Bancroft, Hubert Howe. *The History of Alaska 1730-1885*. San Francisco, CA: A.L. Bancroft & Company 1886.

Barry, Mary J. *A History of Mining on the Kenai Peninsula, Alaska*. Anchorage, AK: MJP BARRY, 1997.

Becker, Ethel A. *Klondike '98*. Portland, OR: 1949.

Berton, Pierre. *Klondike*. Toronto, Canada: McClelland & Stewart Ltd., 1962.

Berton, Pierre. *The Klondike Fever*. Alfred A. Knopf: 1969.

Chaffin, Yule M. *From Koniag to King Crab*. Utah: Desert News Press, 1967.

Chase, Will. *Sourdough Pot*. Kansas City, MO: 1923.

Chooutla Indian School. *Northern Lights*. Carcross, Yukon Territory, Canada: 1913.

Colby, Merle. *A Guide to Alaska*. New York, NY: The MacMillian Company, 1954.

Dall, William H. *Alaska and Its Resources*. Boston, MA: Lee and Shepard, 1870.

Davis, Mary Lee. *Sourdough Gold*. Boston, MA: 1933.

Farrar. *Annexation of Russian America to the United States*. Washington, D.C.: 1937.

Freuchen, Peter. *Law of Larian*.

Goddard. *Indians of the Northwest Coast*. New York, NY: 1945.

Griggs, Robert F. *The Valley of Ten Thousand Smokes*. Washington, D.C.: the National Geographic Society, Washington, D.C.: 1935.

Hamilton, W.R. *Yukon Story*.

Harris, A.C. *Alaska and the Klondike Goldfields*. Chicago, IL: Monroe Book Company, 1897.

Higginson, Ella. *Alaska. New York*, NY: MacMillan Company, 1908.

Hubbard, Father Bernard. *Alaska Odyssey*. Robert Hale Ltd., London, England: 1952.

Hubbard, Father Bernard. *Cradle of the Storms*. Dodd Mead, New York, NY: 1935.

Huntington, James. *On the Edge of Nowhere*.

Ingersoll, Ernest. *Gold Fields of the Klondike*. New York, NY: 1897.

Johnson, Albert. *George Carmack*. Seattle, WA: Epicenter Press Inc., 2001.

Kitchener, L.D. *Flag Over The North*.

Laguna, Frederica de. *Archaeology of Cook Inlet, Alaska*. University of Pennsylvania Press, 1934.

Lathrop, Thornton K. *American Statesman, William Henry Seward*.

Leonard, John W. *Gold Fields of the Klondike*. Chicago, IL: A.N. Marquis and Company, 1897.

Lung, Edward B. *Black Sand and Gold*. New York, NY: 1956.

Lung, Edward B. *Trails to North Star Gold*. Portland, OR: 1969.

Marshall, R. *Arctic Village*.

Mathews, Richard. *The Yukon*. New York, NY: Holt, Rinehart and Winston, 1958.

McLain, J.S. *Alaska and the Yukon*.

Michael, Henry. *Lieutenant Zagoskin's Travels in Russian America, 1842-1844*.

Morgan, Lael. *Good Time Girls*. Seattle, WA: Epicenter Press Inc., 1998.

Morgan, Murray. *One Man's Gold Rush*. Seattle, WA: 1967.

Morgan, Sherwood. Exploration of Alaska, 1865-1900. New Haven, CT: Yale University Press, 1965.

Naske, Claus M. and Slotnick, Herman E. *Alaska, A History of the 49th State*. Grand Rapids, MI: William E. Eerdmans Publishing Company, 1979.

O'Conner, Richard. *High Jinks on the Klondike*. New York, NY: Bobbs-Merrill Company, 1954.

Ogilvie, William. *Early Days on the Yukon*. New York, NY: John Lane Company, 1913.

Osgood, Cornelius. *Contributions to the Ethnograpy of the Kutchin*. New Haven, CT: 1936.

Osgood, Cornelius. *Ethnology of the Tanaina*. New Haven, CT: Yale University Press, 1937.

Osgood, Cornelius. *Ingalik Mental Culture*. New Haven, CT: Yale University Press, 1959.

Oswalt, M. *Alaskan Eskimos*. San Francisco, CA: 1967.

Petroff, Ivan. *10th Census Report, 1880*. Washington, D.C.

Petroff, Ivan. *Report on the Population, Industries, and Resources of Alaska*. Washington: U.S. Printing Office, 1884.

Pierce, Richard A. *Russian America: A Biographical Dictionary*. Fairbanks, AK: The Limestone Press, 1990.

Richard, T.A. *Through the Yukon and Alaska*. San Francisco, CA: 1909.

Schaller, George B. *When the Earth Exploded*. Alaska Book, Ferguson Press, Chicago, IL: 1960.

Seward, Frederick W. *Reminiscences of a War-time Statesman, Seward at Washington as Senator and Secretary of War, and William H. Seward, an Autobiography ... Selections from Letters*.

Sherwood, Morgan. *Alaska and Its History*. Seattle, WA: University of Washington Press, 1967.

Sovereign, A.H. *In Journeyings Often*.

Spencer, R. *North Alaskan Eskimo*. Smithsonian Press, Washington, D.C.: 1969.

Stauter, J.J. *Genius of Seward*. Chicago: J.G. Ferguson Company, 1960.

Stuck, Hudson. *Episcopal Missions in Alaska*.

Stuck, Hudson. *Voyages on the Yukon and its Tributaries*.

Stumer, Harold M. *This was Klondike Fever*. Seattle, WA: Superior Publishing Company, 1978.

Swineford, Alfred P. *Report of the Governor of Alaska*. Sitka: 1886.

Tollemache, Hon. Stratford. *Reminiscences of the Yukon*. Toronto, Canada: 1912.

Underhill, R. *Red Man's Religion*. Chicago, IL: 1965.

U.S. Revenue Cutter Service. *Report of the Operations of the U.S.*

Revenue Steamer Nunivak on the Yukon River Station, Alaska,
1899-1901.

Walden, Arthur T. *A Dog Puncher on the Yukon.* Boston, MA: 1928.

Wickersham, Hon. James. *Old Yukon.* Washington, DC: Washington
Law Book Company, 1938.

Winslow, Kathryn. *Big Pan-Out.* New York, NY: 1951.

Whymper, Frederick. *Travels and Adventures in the Territory of Alaska.*
London, England: 1868.

Periodicals and Newspapers

Alaska Call, March 1960.

Alaska Life, July 1941.

Alaska Life, March 1943.

Alaska Life, August 1944.

Alaska Life, April 1946.

Alaska Life, January 1947.

Alaska Living, October 1968.

Alaska Sportsman, July 1937.

Alaska Sportsman, May 1938.

Alaska Sportsman, May 1951.

Alaska Sportsman, January 1953.

Alaska Sportsman, January 1956.

American Heritage, December 1960.

Island Times, January 1971.

Journal of the West, Vol. 5, 1966.

Klondike News, April 1898.

Kodiak Daily Mirror, June 1971.

National Geographic, June 1963.

Nome News

Orphanage Newsletter [Wood Island], 1905.

Pacific Northern Quarterly, January 1968.

Pathfinder, September 1920.

Pathfinder, October 1922.

PHOTO CREDITS

FOREWORD
P.6, Aunt Phil's Files; p.8, top, University of Alaska Anchorage, National Geographic Society, Katmai Expeditions Collection, UAA-hmc-0186-volume 6-H138; p.8, bottom, University of Alaska Anchorage, Edwin Forbes Glenn Collection, UAA-hmc-0116-series3a-32-1; p.11, Seward Community Library, Sylvia Sexton Collection, SCL-1-798.

CHAPTER 1: UNANSWERED QUESTIONS
P.14, Anchorage Museum of History and Art, Alaska Engineering Commission Collection, AMHA-aec-g934; p.16, Alaska State Library, Summer on the Thetis Collection, ASL-P27-113; p.17, Anchorage Museum of History and Art, Crary-Henderson Collection, AMHA-b62-1-579; p.19, University of Alaska Fairbanks, Cordelia L. M. Noble Collection, UAF-1973-203-22; p.21, University of Alaska Anchorage, Thomas W. Benham Collection, UAA-hmc-0069-cUnalaska-8; p.23, Alaska State Library Place File, ASL-P01-4184.

CHAPTER 2: COPING WITH THE UNKNOWN
P.26, Alaska State Library, Case and Draper Collection, ASL-P39-0782; p.29, Alaska State Library, Lyman Knapp Collection, ASL-P438-38; p.30, Alaska State Library, William Norton Collection, ASL-P226-64;

CHAPTER 3: ALASKA'S CHANGING LANDSCAPE
P.35, Anchorage Museum of History and Art, General Photograph File, AMHA-b92-4-15; p.36, University of Alaska Fairbanks, Vertical File Small Photograph Collections, UAF-1999-222-2; p.38, University of Washington, Harriman Alaska Expedition Collection, HAR169.

CHAPTER 4: EARTHQUAKES FORM LANDSCAPE
P.40, University of Alaska Fairbanks, J. Bernard Moore Family Collection, UAF-1976-35-36; p.41, Alaska State Library, Lyman E. Knapp Collection, ASL-P438-24; p.43, Alaska State Library Place File, ASL-P01-2529; p.44, University of Alaska Fairbanks, Vertical File Photograph Collection, UAF-1972-152-73.

CHAPTER 5: WHEN THE U.S. WAS BEING BORN ...
P.45, Alaska State Library, A Voyage to the Pacific Ocean by James Cook, PCA-20-57; P.47, Alaska State Library Portrait File, ASL-James Cook; p.48, Alaska State Library Portrait File, ALS-P01-2603.

CHAPTER 6: NATIVES ATTACK RUSSIAN FORTS
P.49, Penny postcard/E.W. Merrill photographer; p.50, University of Washington, Alaska and Western Canada Collection, AWC0322; p.53, Alaska State Library, Wickersham State Historic Site Collection, ASL-P277-17-12; p.54, Frontiers.loc.gov; p.56, Alaska State Library, George A. Parks Collection, ASL-P240-210.

CHAPTER 7: LITTLE-KNOWN STORIES

P.58, Anchorage Museum of History and Art, General Photograph File, AMHA-b77-107-25; p.59, W. Kinsler Technology, New York and St. Clair Ice Machine; p.60, University of Alaska Anchorage, National Geographic Society, Katmai Expedition Collection, UAA-hmc-0186-volume1-3750.

CHAPTER 8: LAST SHOT OF CIVIL WAR

P.64, U.S. Navy No. NH42279.

CHAPTER 9: SEWARD'S FOLLY BECOMES A U.S. TREASURE

P.66, Alaska State Library Portrait Files, ASL-01-4050; p.67, Alaska State Library Portrait Files, Charles Sumner; p.68, University of Washington, Alaska and Western Canada Collection, AWC0640; p.70, Alaska State Library, William A. Kelly Collection, ASL-P427-26; p.71, Alaska State Library Portrait Files, ASL-P01-3775; p.72, top, Alaska State Library, Early Prints Photograph Collection, ASL-297-251; p.72, bottom, Alaska State Library, Early Prints Photograph Collection, ASL-297-113; p.73, Library of Congress; p.74, Alaska State Library, Winter and Pond Collection, ASL-87-1512; p.75, Alaska State Library Place File, ASL-P01-1565; p.77, Library of Congress; p.78, Alaska State Library, Winter and Pond Collection, ASL-P87-161; p.80, Rare Books, Special Collections and Preservation, University of Rochester Library; p.81, National Police Gazette, Contemporary Woodcut Engravings; p.82, University of Rochester Library, Dr. John K. Lattimer, "Kennedy and Lincoln: Medical and Ballistic Comparisons of Their Assassinations."

CHAPTER 10: APOSTLE TO THE NORTH

P.84, University of Alaska Fairbanks, Historical Files, UAF-77-243; P.85, Anchorage Museum of History and Art, O.D. Goetze Collection, AMHA-b01-41-66; p.87, University of Alaska Fairbanks, Lawyer and Cora Rivenburg Collection, UAF-1994-70-279; p.88, Museum of Canada, Yukon Archives; p.89, Anchorage Museum of History and Art, General Photograph File, AMHA-b79-2-4819; p.90, Museum of Canada, Yukon Archives.

CHAPTER 11: ALASKA'S MYSTERIOUS FIRST CENSUS-TAKER

P.92, University of Alaska Fairbanks, Selid Bassoc Collection, UAF-1964-92-517; p. 94, University of Alaska Fairbanks, Selid Bassoc Collection, UAF-1964-92-539; p.95, Anchorage Museum of History and Art, Crary-Henderson Collection, AMHA-b62-1-571; p.97, Alaska State Library Place File, ASL-01-1340; p.99, Alaska State Library, Winter and Pond Collection, ASL-P87-1482.

CHAPTER 12: GOLD FOUND IN SOUTHEAST

P.100, Alaska State Library Portrait File, ASL-01-1155; p.101, Alaska State Library, William H. Partridge Collection, ASL-P88-90; p.102, University of Alaska Anchorage, Richard Tighe Harris Family Collection, UAA-hmc-0131-series5b-59-2; p.103, Alaska State Library, Winter and Pond Collection, ASL-P87-350; p.105, Alaska State Library, Winter and Pond Collection, ASL-P87-570; p.106, Alaska State Library, Winter and Pond Collection, ASL-87-385.

CHAPTER 13: EXPLORING THE NILE OF ALASKA

P.108, Alaska State Library Documents, "A Summer in Alaska," by Frederick Schwatka, ASL-F912.Y9-S521-1894-p65; p.109, Alaska State Library Portrait Files, ASL-P01-2594; p.110, Alaska State Library, Arthur C. Pillsbury Collection, ASL-P230-5; p.112, University of Alaska Fairbanks, Dr. Ernest A. Cook Collection, UAF-2003-109-249.

CHAPTER 14: OLD JOHN BREMNER

P.114, University of Alaska Fairbanks, Vertical File Historical Photo, UAF 77-164-1; p.115, Anchorage Museum of History and Art, Crary-Henderson Collection, AMHA-b62-1-911; p.116, University of Alaska Fairbanks, Lawyer and Cora Rivenburg Collection, UAF-1994-70-80; p.118, University of Alaska Anchorage, Estelle and Philip Garges Collection, UAA-hmc-0381-series2-58-6; p.119, University of Alaska Fairbanks, J. Bernard Moore Collection, UAF-1976-35-30; p.120, University of Alaska Fairbanks, Mr. and Mrs. Gregory Kokrine Collection, UAF-87-2a.

CHAPTER 15: RICH NAMES ALONG THE KOYUKUK

P.123, University of Washington, Eric A. Hegg Collection, HEG253; p.124, top, University of Alaska Fairbanks, Lawyer and Cora Rivenburg Collection, UAf-1994-70-337; p.124, bottom, University of Alaska Fairbanks, Lawyer and Cora Rivenburg Collection, UAF-1994-70-351; p.126, Alaska State Library, Skinner Foundation Collection, ASL-P44-3-15; p.128, Alaska State Library, Dr. Daniel S. Neuman Collection, ASL-P307-30; p.129, University of Alaska Fairbanks, Dr. Ernest A. Cook Collection, UAF-2003-109-243; p.130, Alaska State Library, Skinner Foundation Collection, ASL-P44-3-150.

CHAPTER 16: ALASKA'S SECOND GOLD RUSH

P.135, Anchorage Museum of History and Art, General Photograph File, AMHA-b74-4-8; p.136, Anchorage Museum of History and Art, Crary-Henderson Collection, AMHA-b62-1-689; p.137, University of Alaska Anchorage, Edwin Forbes Glenn Collection, UAA-hmc-0116-series3a-11-1; p.138, top, Alaska State Library, William R. Norton Collection, ASL-P226-481; p.138, bottom, Alaska State Library, William R. Norton Collection, ASL-P226-473; p.139, Museum of Canada, Yukon Archives No. 133; p.141, Anchorage Museum of History and Art, General Photograph Files, AMHA-b97-6-3.

CHAPTER 17: DREAMS OF SALMON TURN TO GOLD

P.144, University of Washington, Eric A. Hegg Collection, HEG407; p.145, University of Washington, Asahel Curtis Collection, CUR1618; p.146, top, National Museum of Canada, Yukon Archives; p.146, bottom, Museum of Canada, Yukon Archives; p.147, University of Washington, Eric Hegg Collection, HEG208; p.148, University of Washington, Frank LaRoche Collection, LAR222; p.150, Museum of Canada, Yukon Archives No. 54; p.151, Museum of Canada, Yukon Archives; p.152, University of Washington, Eric A. Hegg Collection, HEG 580; p.153, University of Washington, Eric A. Hegg Collection, HEG735; p.155, University of Washington, Alaska and Western Canada Collection, AWC812; p.156, Museum of Canada, Yukon Archives; p.157, University of Washington, James Albert Johnson Collection, Yukon Archives No. 21; p.158, University of Washington, Asahel Curtis Collection, CUR1360; p.159, Museum of Canada, Yukon Archives; p. 160, Museum of

Canada, Yukon Archives No. 7783; p.161, Anchorage Museum of History and Art, General Photograph File, AMHA-b62-1-2241.

CHAPTER 18: LUCKIEST MAN ON THE KLONDIKE

P.164, University of Washington, Asahel Curtis Collection, CUR1449; p.165, Alaska State Library, Dr. Daniel S. Neuman Collection, ASL-P307-116; p.166, Aunt Phil's Files; p.167, University of Washington, Eric A. Hegg Collection, HEG670; p.168, University of Washington, Alaska and Western Canada Collection, AWC501; p.169, University of Washington, Asahel Curtis Collection, CUR1482; p.170, University of Alaska Fairbanks, Mary Whalen Collection, UAF-75-84-377; p.173, Aunt Phil's Files.

CHAPTER 19: DAWSON IS BORN

P.174, University of Washington, Eric A. Hegg Collection, HEG457; p.175, University of Washington, Eric A. Hegg Collection, HEG090; p.176, University of Washington, Eric A. Hegg Collection, HEG617; p.178, University of Alaska Fairbanks, Mary Whalen Collection, UAF-75-84-241; p.179, University of Washington, Eric A. Hegg Collection, HEG408; p.180, University of Alaska Fairbanks, Barrett Willoughby Collection, UAF-1972-116-34; p.181, University of Washington, Eric A. Hegg Collection, HEG092; p.183, University of Washington, Eric A. Heg Collection, HEG527; p.184, University of Washington, Eric A. Hegg Collection, HEG677; p.185, University of Alaska Fairbanks, Selid Bassoc Collection, UAF-64-92-17; p.186, University of Washington, Eric A. Hegg Collection, HEG638; p.188, University of Alaska Fairbanks, Barrett Willoughby Collection, UAF-1972-116-335; p.190, Dawson City Museum, Yukon Archives; p.191, University of Washington, Frank LaRoche Collection, LAR168; p.192, University of Washington, Alaska and Western Canada Collection, AWC0932; p.193, top, University of Alaska Fairbanks, J.Bernard Moore Collection, UAF-1976-35-55; p.193, bottom, Museum of Canada, Yukon Archives.

CHAPTER 20: ST. MICHAEL AWAKENS

P.195, Museum of Canada, Yukon Archives; p.196, Seattle Post Intelligencer; P.197, University of Washington, Wilse Photo 531; p.198, Alaska State Library, Skinner Foundation, ASL-P44-9-88; p.199, University of Washington, Frank H. Nowell Collection, NOW210; p. 200, Anchorage Museum of History and Art, General Photograph File, AMHA-b65-18-38; p.201, Museum of Canada, Yukon Archives No. 118.

CHAPTER 21: WHITE PASS AND CHILKOOT PASS TRAILS

P.203, University of Washington, Eric A. Hegg Collection, HEG444; p.204, University of Washington, Eric A. Hegg Collection, HEG117; p.205, University off Washington, Alaska and Western Canada, AWC442; p.206, University of Washington, Eric A. Hegg Collection, HEG611; p.207, University of Alaska Fairbanks, George and Lilly Clark Collection, UAF-1986-109-2; p.208, University of Washington, Eric A. Hegg Collection, HEG241; p.209, University of Washington, Frank LaRoche Collection, LAR189; p.211, University of Washington, Eric A. Hegg, HEG629; p. 212, Aunt Phil's Files; p.213, University of Washington, Eric A. Hegg Collection, HEG695; p.214, University of Washington, Eric A. Hegg, HEG159; p.215, University of Washington, Alaska and Western Canada Collection, AWC0846; p.216, University of Washington, Eric A. Hegg, HEG149.

CHAPTER 22: TRAIL TO GOLD PHOTO ESSAY

P.218, National Park Service map; p.219, University of Washington, Frank LaRoche Collection, LAR258; p.220, top, Alaska State Library, Skinner Foundation Collection, ASL-P44-9-51; p.220, bottom, University of Washington, Wilheim Hester Collection, HES347;

STIKINE RIVER ROUTE

P. 221, National Park Service map; p.222, University of Washington, Frank LaRoche Collection, LAR115; P.223, top, University of Washington, Frank LaRoche Collection, LAR299; p.223, bottom, University of Washington, Alaska Western Canada Collection, AWC1034; p.224, top, University of Washington, Asahel Curtis Collection, CUR1435; p.224, bottom, University of Washington, Eric A. Hegg Collection, HEG206.

WHITE PASS TRAIL ROUTE

P.225, top, University of Washington, Frank LaRoche Collection, LAR109; p.225, bottom, University of Washington, Alaska Western Canada Collection, AWC0347; p.226, top, University of Washington, Eric A. Hegg Collection, HEG155; p.226, bottom, University of Washington, Frank LaRoche Collection, LAR221; p.227, University of Washington, Asahel Curtis Collection, CUR1447; p.228, top, Eric A. Hegg Collection, HEG130; p.228, bottom, University of Washington, Eric A. Hegg, HEG184.

CHILKOOT PASS TRAIL ROUTE

P.229, University of Alaska Fairbanks, J. Bernard Moore Collection, UAF-1976-35-43; p.230, University of Washington, Frank LaRoche Collection, LAR202; p.231 University of Washington, Frank LaRoche Collection, LAR207; p.232, top, University of Washington, Frank LaRoche Collection, LAR208; p.232, bottom, University of Washington, Alaska and Western Canada Collection, AWC837; p.233, Alaska State Library, Arthur Clarence Pillsbury Collection, ASL-P230-08; p.234, top, University of Washington, Frank LaRoche Collection, LAR211; p.234, bottom, University of Washington, Frank LaRoche Collection, LAR226; p.235, University of Washington, Eric A. Hegg Collection, HEG135; p.236, top, University of Washington, Eric A. Hegg Collection, HEG001; p.236, bottom, University of Washington, Eric A. Hegg, HEG054; p.237, University of Washington, Frank LaRoche Collection, LAR238; p.238, top, University of Washington, Eric A. Hegg Collection, HEG629; p.238, bottom, University of Washington, Eric A. Hegg Collection, HEG169; p.239, top, University of Washington, Eric A. Hegg Collection, HEG119; p.239, bottom, University of Washington, Eric A. Hegg, HEG356; p.240, top, University of Washington, Asahel Curtis Collection, CUR1431; p.240, bottom, Alaska State Library, Wickersham State Historic Site, ASL-P277-1-35; p.241, University of Washington, Alaska and Western Canada Collection, AWC1020; p.242, top, University of Alaska Fairbanks, J. Bernard Moore Collection, UAF-1976-35-85; p.242, bottom, University of Washington, Frank LaRoche Collection, LAR214; p.243, University of Washington, Michael Meed Collection, MEE173; p.244, top, University of Washington, Eric A. Hegg, HEG560; p.244, bottom, University of Washington, Eric A. Hegg, HEG247; p.245, top, University of Washington, Asahel Curtis, CUR1439; p.245, bottom, University of Washington, Alaska and Western Canada Collection, AWC866.

STAMPEDERS STRUGGLE IN GOLD FIELDS
P.246, University of Washington, Alaska and Western Canada Collection, AWC869; p.247, top, University of Washington, Eric A. Hegg, HEG038; p.247, bottom, Museum of Canada, Yukon Archives No. 9156; p.248, top, University of Washington, Frank H. Nowell Collection, NOW274; p.248, bottom, University of Washington, Alaska Western Canada Collection, AWC366; p.249, top, University of Washington, Michael Meed Collection, MEE205; p.249, bottom, University of Washington, Eric A. Hegg, HEG386; p.250, top, University of Washington, Michael Meed Collection, MEE51; p.250, bottom, University of Washington, Alaska and Western Canada Collection, AWC75; p.251, University of Washington, Eric A. Hegg, HEG722; p.253, University of Washington, Eric A. Hegg Collection, HEG251.

CHAPTER 23: JACK DALTON CREATES TOLL ROAD
P.255, University of Alaska Fairbanks, Charles Burnell Collection, UAF-58-1026-180N; p.256, University of Alaska Fairbanks, Historical Photo, UAF-77-32-4.

CHAPTER 24: SEA CAPTAIN STIFLES MUTINY
P.259, University of Alaska Fairbanks, William Sale Collection, UAF-1979-106-1; p.260, University of Washington, Harriman Alaska Expedition Collection, HAR221; p.262, Alaska State Library, Wickersham State Historic Site Collection, ASL-P277-1-9.

CHAPTER 25: SOAPY SMITH HEADS TO SKAGWAY
P.264, University of Alaska Fairbanks, J. Bernard Moore Family Collection, UAF-1976-35-53; p.265, Alaska State Library, Case and Draper Collection, ASL-P39-843; p.267, top, University of Washington, Eric A. Hegg Collection, HEG721; p.267, bottom, University of Washington, Alaska and Western Canada Collection, AWC0348.

CHAPTER 26: MINERS STAMPEDE TO NOME
P.268, Alaska State Library, Alaska Purchase Centennial Collection, ASL-P20-88; p.269, top, University of Washington, Alaska and Western Canada Collection, AWC0264; p.269, bottom, Alaska State Library, Alfred G. Simmer Collection, ASL-P137-038; p.270, University of Washington, Wilhelm Hester Collection, HES109; p.271, Anchorage Museum of History and Art, O.D. Goetze Collection, AMHA-b01-41-37; p.272, Alaska State Library, Wickersham State Historic Site, ASL-P277-9-26; p.273, Anchorage Museum of History and Art, O.D. Goetze Collection, AMHA-b01-41-8; p.274, University of Washington, Eric A. Hegg Collection, HEG270; p.275, University of Washington, Alaska and Western Canada Collection, AWC1079; p.277, Anchorage Museum of History and Art, O.D. Goetze Collection, AMHA-b01-41-267; p.278, www.city-data.com; p.279, University of Washington, Eric A. Hegg, HEG262; p.280, top, University of Washington, Alaska and Western Canada Collection, AWC0011; p.280, bottom, University of Washington, Frank H. Nowell Collection, NOW155.

CHAPTER 27: SISTERS OF PROVIDENCE
P.281, University of Washington, Eric A. Hegg Collection, HEG428; p.282, Sisters of Providence Archives, Seattle; p.283, Sisters of Providence Archives, Seattle; p.284, Sisters of Providence Archives, Seattle; p.285, University of Washington, Frank H. Nowell Collection, NOW185; p.286, Alaska State Library, Paul Sincic Collection, ASL-P75-431; p.287, Sisters of Providence Archives Seattle.

CHAPTER 28: NATIVES AND THE RUSH FOR GOLD

P.290, University of Washington, Frank LaRoche Collection, LAR185; p.291, top, University of Washington, Frank LaRoche Collection, LAR188; p.291, bottom, University of Washington, Frank LaRoche Collection, LAR215; p.292, top, University of Washington, Alaska Western Canada Collection, AWC0125; p.292, bottom, University of Washington, Alaska Western Canada Collection, AWC0020; p.293, University of Washington, Frank H. Nowell Collection, NOW055; p.295, University of Washington, Frank LaRoche Collection, LAR216; p.296, Anchorage Museum of History and Art, O.D. Goetze Collection, AMHA-b01-41-104a; p.297, University of Washington, William Meed Collection, MEE055; p.298, University of Washington, William Meed Collection, MEE070; p.299, top, University of Washington, Alaska Western Canada Collection, AWC0896; p.299, bottom, University of Washington, Eric A. Hegg Collection HEG710.

CHAPTER 29: RICHEST NATIVE WOMAN IN THE NORTH

P.301, University of Washington, Eric A. Hegg Collection, HEG284; p.302, Courtesy Sinrock Mary's great-granddaughter Jodi Newell; p.303, University of Washington, Asahel Curtis Collection, CUR1495;

CHAPTER 30: BIRTH OF FORT YUKON

P.305, University of Washington, Eric A. Hegg Collection, HEG717; p.306, Hudson's Bay Company Canada; p.307, Courtesy U.S. Fish and Wildlife Service; p.308, Alaska State Library, Wickersham State Historic Site Photographs, ASL-PCA-277-017-038; p.309, University of Washington, Eric A. Hegg Collection, HEG320.

CHAPTER 31: FAIRBANKS STARTED FROM RICH BANKS

P.310, University of Washington, Alaska Western Canada Collection, AWC1134.

CHAPTER 32: BLUE PARKA BANDIT

P.314, University of Alaska Fairbanks, Walter and Lilian Phillips Collection, UAF-1985-72-1; p.315, University of Alaska Fairbanks, Albert J. Johnson Collection, UAF-89-166-635; p.316, University of Alaska Fairbanks, Albert J. Johnson Collection, UAF-89-166-658; p.317, University of Washington, Asahel Curtis, CUR594; p.318, University of Alaska Fairbanks, Selid Bassoc Collection, UAF-64-92-444; p.320, Photo by Laurel Bill from Alaska State Troopers Museum in Anchorage; p.321, Alaska State Library, Skinner Foundation Collection, ASL-P44-09-005; p.323, University of Alaska Anchorage, D.S. Clark Collection, UAA-hmc-0614-22a; p.324, University of Washington, Asahel Curtis Collection, CUR592; p.326, University of Washington, Asahel Curtis Collection, CUR595.

PREVIEW AUNT PHIL'S TRUNK:VOLUME 2

P.338, top, Aunt Phil's files; p.338, bottom, NOAA; p.339, University of Washington, Eric A. Hegg Collection, HEG425; p.340, top, NOAA; p.340, bottom, University of Alaska Fairbanks Museum Classification UA91-017-001; p.341, University of Washington, John Twaites Collection, THW154; p.342, University of Washington, Alaska-Yukon-Pacific-Exposition, AYP145; p.343, Library of Congress; p.344, National Park Service.

Preview of Aunt Phil's Trunk: Volume 2

Scheduled to be on bookstore shelves in Spring 2007, "Aunt Phil's Trunk: Volume 2" will feature more entertaining stories about Alaska's colorful past. Here's a preview of some of those tales.

Alaska's first law officer
Alaska's first law officer in the Interior knew a thing or two about the criminal element. Frank Canton, appointed deputy marshal for Circle in February 1898, had served with distinction as a peace officer in Wyoming and Oklahoma Territory. He'd also escaped from prison while serving time for a litany of offenses, including murder.

Tombstone temporarily transplanted in Alaska
Many of those hardy gunslingers and prospectors who made Tombstone a household word in the late 1800s, landed in Alaska and the Yukon after the demise of the Arizona city. Among them were Wyatt Earp and John Clum.

Wyatt Earp, right, arrived in Nome in 1897.

A large crowd gathers outside of "The Second Class, the only second-class saloon in Alaska," owned by Wyatt Earp in Nome in 1901.

Gold Rush brings postal system north

In 1891 John P. Clum went to Washington to start a 20-year career as a postal inspector. This service would take him to all parts of the United States, and in 1898 to the Territory of Alaska, where he organized the Territorial Postal System. He retired from the Postal Service in 1910.

Sourdough preacher painter settles in Cordova

One Alaska artist's work aptly captures the epic struggle of sourdough days, portraying that historic period when pioneer men and women conquered a rugged wilderness and opened the Alaska Frontier. The hunched backs of prospectors, bowed under heavy packs; the white, desolate tundra; powerful, winding rivers; the frigid majesty of snowy mountains, and small fishing boats boldly defying the mighty oceans fill Eustace Paul Ziegler's canvases.

Eustace Ziegler painted Tanana Woman and Dog, oil on board, in 1939.

The day Alaska turned dark

Earthquakes creating the islands around Bogoslof and giant waves in Lituya Bay are evidence that Alaska tends to do things in a big way. And before one of the most violent earthquakes in the nation's history shook things up on Good Friday 1964, another earthshaking event occurred.

On June 6, 1912, the earth exploded. People living within a radius of several hundred miles were given a taste of what hell fire and brimstone of Biblical teachings might be like.

Mail steamer *Dora* arrives in Seward after passing through the eruption of Katmai Volcano near Kodiak Island on June 6, 1912. The clerk on the mail ship vividly described the experience as the ship crossed the area of falling ash.

"... lurid flashes of lightning glared continually around the ship while a constant boom of thunder increased the horror of the inferno raging around us ... we might as well have been miles above the surface of the water ... birds floundered, crying wildly through space and fell helpless to the deck."

Trail-blazer on wheels

On July 29, 1913, one of Alaska's trail-blazers started a historic journey – the first automobile trip over the wagon trail from Fairbanks to Valdez.

But that wasn't Robert E. "Bobby" Sheldon's first experience with a motorized vehile. Sheldon, who'd never seen an automobile, also built the first car in Alaska. As he described his creation:

"All I knew about them was what I read in papers from the States. I was interested in mechanics, and being on the night shift at the Skagway power house, I had considerable time to think it over. It was my job to make all kinds of emergency repairs on the equipment. My funds were limited, but I finally located four buggy wheels and built a frame over them. ..."

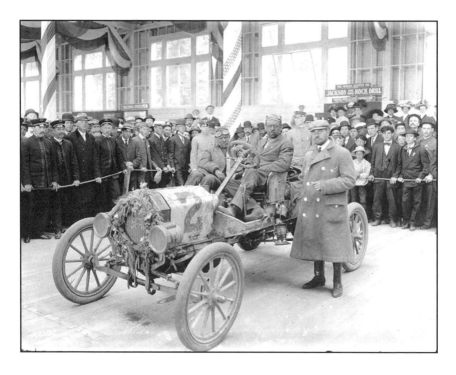

This Ford Model "T" car No. 2 was on display at the Alaska-Yukon-Pacific Exposition in Seattle in June 1909.

Black fog over Barrow

When rescuers arrived on the scene of an airplane crash near Point Barrow on Aug. 15, 1935, they found Will Rogers dead. A typewriter recovered in the wreckage had Rogers' unfinished last "piece for the papers," and the final word he'd typed was "death."

But Rogers didn't seem to have had a premonition that his trip to Alaska would end in disaster. In an interview in Portland, Oregon, a short time before the

WILL ROGERS
IN VAUDEVILLE.

tragedy, he was asked, "When are you going to write a book on your life?"

"I don't know," Rogers replied. "I ain't near dead enough yet. One publisher has been after me a long time to write my memoirs. But, shucks, you got to be old and pretty near dead to have anything to look back on. I'm a long ways from being dead. Feel just as frisky as a colt!"

Mount St. Elias, tough every foot of the way

Mount St. Elias, the first point sighted by white man on the mainland of Alaska in 1741, has proved a mighty challenge to mountaineers. Only a handful of climbers have conquered it in the 265 years since the Dane Vitus Bering discovered and named it for Russia.

English explorers George Dixon and James Cook noted the mighty mountain, too, in their explorations, and in 1786, Jean-

---

François de Galoup, Comte de La Perouse's astronomer, Joseph Lepaute Dagelet, calculated its altitude at 12,672 feet. A few years later, Spanish explorer Alejandro Malaspina determined its altitude at 17,851 feet, remarkably near its true height, at 18,024 feet as decided upon by Coast Survey Triangulation in 1892.

These and many more stories highlighting Alaska's rich past fill the pages of "Aunt Phil's Trunk" Volume 2 and Volume 3.